THE TRUCKIE WHO LOVED TRAINS

THE BIOGRAPHY OF KEN THOMAS
FOUNDER OF THOMAS NATIONWIDE TRANSPORT

T|N|T

BY DAVID WILCOX

Ken Thomas

THE BIOGRAPHY OF KEN THOMAS

1913-1997

The man who made a huge contribution to the development of transport in Australia in the 20th century.

From a one-truck start in 1946, within 25 years he built TNT to be the largest transport company in Australia.

BY DAVID WILCOX

Printed in Australia

First Printing, 2013
Second Edition, 2014
Third Edition, 2015
International B&W POD Edition, 2016

ISBN 9780646595702 (pbk)
ISBN 9781925281620 (int POD)
ISBN 9781925281637 (ebk)

National Library of Australia Cataloguing in Publication data.

David Wilcox 1935-
davwilcox@bigpond.com

Biography Kenneth William Thomas
Land Transport. TNT

www.thetruckiewholovedtrains.com

Acknowledgements

TNT Logo used with permission of TNT Express

Photos: Thomas family, TNT magazine, Freight Notes, NSW State Library, Harden Historical Society, Sydney Morning Herald, A.R.H.S. (NSW), A.R.H.S. (SA), Catchpoint —May 1995 Bob Grant, NSW RTM, Roundhouse, Truck & Bus Transportation, NSWGR, Bob McKillop N.A.A. (30451747), Vision Valley, Road Transport Historical Society, Brian Bertwistle, Gordon Barton—biography by Everingham.

Design by Perfect Miistake Designs—perfecmiistakedesigns@gmail.com

Printed by WHO Printing, Mayfield West, NSW.

CONTENTS

Introduction

Foreword

INTRODUCTION

This is the story of an evolution. It covers the dramatic change in Australian transport over the 25 years after World War Two.

In that time so many important changes occurred.

They include the sorting out of the railway gauge problems; the dieselisation of the railways; the Hughes and Vale road tax decision; the arrival of containers and roll-on roll-off shipping. Best of all, the marriage of road and rail freight operations.

These things did not happen by nature taking its course; they happened because driven men could see a better way. One of the leaders of these men was Ken Thomas.

I am fortunate because my brother Murray chose as his bride Christina, whose aunt was Ken's wife Anne. I first met Ken at Murray and Christina's wedding in 1959. I worked in the transport industry selling the services of a Thomas competitor, so I knew how Ken was setting the pace.

Ken realised his story was worth recording. In December 1992 in a letter to Bill Martin, a long-time friend and colleague, he said, "I am thinking of writing a history of Thomas Nationwide Transport, from 1946 to 1972. That 25-year period was a red-blooded, gutsy period, abounding in good stories. People keep nudging me to write the story and supplement it with interesting photos. I know more about it than anyone, but only to 1972."

Ken never got to write his story, and his natural modesty would probably have restricted the descriptions of his own achievements, which can best be recounted by others with hindsight vision.

In 2008 I first visited the Road Transport Historical Society Hall of Fame at Alice Springs, and was overwhelmed with the display mounted there with vehicles, men, and a few women who had contributed to the development of Australian transport. There was nothing about Ken Thomas or TNT, so I resolved to correct that deficiency. That was a challenge to me.

Ken's family supported the idea to prepare a nomination of him in the Hall of Fame, and five of them were there for the award in August 2012. Daughter Megan, although seriously ill and in great pain, made the trip and was thrilled with the recognition of her father. She passed away seven weeks later.

What started as a simple citation grew to become this book.

This is a story about Australian transport in the 20th century, with a cast of thousands, and the star of the show is Kenneth William Thomas.

David Wilcox

FOREWORD

Each year the Road Transport Historical Society Inc. calls for nominations of people who have made a significant contribution to the Australian Road Transport Industry to be recognised and honoured, by induction to the Shell Rimula Wall of Fame, at the Alice Springs Transport Museum.

In 2012, Ken was nominated, and then admitted at an induction on 25th August. The nomination was made with the support of Ken's family by David Wilcox, with Milton Morris as referee. Milton was the New South Wales Minister for Transport from 1965 to 1975.

The citation read:

Ken Thomas started in the transport industry in 1946 with the purchase of a five ton International truck. He could have little realised at that time that his name would go on to be a household name the world over. Ken had gained two university degrees in the 1930s, so entered the industry with a wide range of business skills. Neverless, it was tough in those early years and Ken employed a driver for the first truck while he held down another job for the first two years while he got the business going.

Initially Ken traded as K.W. Thomas, but later formed a company. In 1961, just 15 years later, the company listed on the stock exchange as Thomas Nationwide Transport, better known as TNT. The company still exists and has services world wide. Ken found that long distance interstate road transport was the best option despite the restrictions with road tax and government permits. He believed in having branch offices rather than agents, and by 1950 had employees in Melbourne, Adelaide and Brisbane as well as his home base of Sydney. Ken Thomas was the undisputed leader in the interstate hauling fraternity.

Ken was instrumental in the formation of the Long Distance Hauliers Association; he was the foundation vice-president and a trustee for some years. The Association led the fight against interstate road tax and helped finance the Hughes and Vale challenge to section 92 of the Constitution, which was won in the Privy Council.

Ironically Ken was the son of an engine driver. He had respect for rail transport and did not regard it as the enemy, because it had an important role in the Australian economy. Ken's initiative and enthusiasm led, in 1952, to the bulk loading scheme with the railway systems. From there extensive coordination activities, such as containerisation, piggy back, and flexi-vans made a huge difference to the efficiency of rail transport. Australia led the world in this field.

In both forms of transport Ken gave Australian companies door-to-door, fast and frequent service. He was the first to develop a freight note that gave all the information needed and became the invoice; unheard of previously, but other companies quickly followed and it is now a standard operating procedure in all freight businesses.

Ken Thomas led the TNT organisation until 1972. He died in 1997, leaving Australia with one of the most cost-effective and efficient land transport industries in the world.

The family of Ken Thomas were thrilled with the Hall of Fame Award.

From Left: Daughters, Megan on the left, Elizabeth in front, with son, Rhody, accept the Hall of Fame plaque from Liz Martin.

KEN THOMAS

Ken Thomas started in the transport industry in 1946 with the purchase of a 5 ton International truck. He could have little realised at the time that his name would go on to become a household name the world over. Ken had gained two university degrees in the 1930s so had entered the industry with a wide range of business skills. Never-the-less, it was tough in those early years and Ken employed a driver on his first truck while he held down another job for two years to get the business going.

Initially Ken traded as K W Thomas but later formed a company. In 1961, just 15 years later, the company listed on the stock exchange as Thomas Nationwide Transport, better known today as TNT. The company still exists and has services worldwide.

Ken found long distance interstate road transport to be the best option despite the restrictions with road tax and government permits. He believed in having branch offices rather than agents and by 1950 had employees in Melbourne, Brisbane and Adelaide as well as in his home base of Sydney.

Ken Thomas was an undisputed leader in developing the interstate hauling fraternity. He was instrumental in the formation of the Long Distance Hauliers Association and was the foundation vice-president and then the trustee for some years. The Association led the fight against interstate road tax and helped finance the Hughes and Vale challenge to section 92 of the constitution which was won in the Privy Council.

Ironically, Ken Thomas was the son of an engine driver. He had a respect for rail transport and did not regard it as the enemy because it had an important role in the Australian economy. Ken's initiative and enthusiasm led, in 1952, to the bulk loading scheme with the railway systems. From there extensive coordination activities, such as containerisation, piggy-back and flexi-vans, made a huge difference to the efficiency of rail transport. Australia led the world in this field.

In both forms of transport Ken gave Australian companies door to door, fast and frequent services. He was the first to develop a freight note that gave all the information needed which became the invoice, unheard of previously but other companies quickly followed and it is now a standard operating procedure in all freight businesses.

Ken Thomas led the TNT organisation until 1972. He died in 1997 leaving Australia with one of the most cost effective and efficient land transport industries in the world.

Inducted 2012

SHELL RIMULA WALL OF FAME
INDUCTED – 2012
NATIONAL ROAD TRANSPORT HALL OF FAME

The plaque presented to the Thomas family

MY THANKS

This book is dedicated to Dorothy, the love of my life, my best friend and sternest critic. Her interest and encouragement has been consistent, and for 14 months she has patiently accepted that the time I have devoted to Ken Thomas has been at the expense of time with her.

There are many who have helped with the research and writing. Ken's family, Elizabeth, Rhody, Megan and Gavin have given enthusiastic support and appreciation. They knew that Ken's life and work had not been fairly and adequately recorded, so loaned Ken's papers for research. Megan's terminal illness did not dampen her enthusiasm, but it deprived her of a view of the finished product.

My brothers, Murray and Graham Wilcox have advised, supported, criticised and asked questions, as only brothers on good terms can do. Their contribution has been valuable.

Other friends whose advice and support have helped are, Rebecca Layfield, Wayne Barrett, Paul Cotter, Douglas Stuart, Graham Black, and Ian McNeil.

Special mention must be made of Liz Martin of the Australian Transport Museum at Alice Springs for her interest and encouragement. Then the co-operation and stimulus of Lorraine Brown, Robyn Atherton and Darren Sargent of the Harden Historical Society have also been important.

The research work has been much easier because of the information given, and the interest shown, by so many past TNT staff. Most of their stories have been included and attributed to them.

I was very fortunate to meet Daniel Cummings only a few months ago. He was just the person I needed. Daniel is a professional designer, and his work is very apparent in the book.

The demand for the book has led to a second edition in January 2014. The success was set off by the launch of the first edition by the Hon. Tim Fischer AC, at a dinner arranged by the Harden- Murrumburrah Historical Society, which also marked the Centenary of Ken's birth.

While many have enthusiastically promoted the book to their friends and contacts, particular thanks have to be given to the people at TNT Express. Their interest and assistance ranges from a very efficient and reliable service for delivery of the books, to the practice of giving copies to their staff who have earned long service awards. Having met and had dealings with dozens of TNT people, I believe they all faithfully reflect and follow the principles and philosophy of Ken Thomas.

Writing this book has been a memorable and satisfying experience for me. I hope reading the book will be just that for all who read it.

David Wilcox

THE TRUCKIE WHO LOVED TRAINS

BY DAVID WILCOX

"AUSTRALIA HAS DEVELOPED THE MOST EFFICIENT TRANSPORT SYSTEM IN THE WORLD."

—*KEN THOMAS*

"KEN WAS A TRUE LEADER OF THE TRANSPORT INDUSTRY, WHO HAS NOT BEEN RECOGNISED AS HE SHOULD BE."

—*MILTON MORRIS, NSW MINISTER OF TRANSPORT (1965-1975)*

THE HARDEN BOY

It was all falling into place. Ken Thomas was about to collect his new truck.

He would be working for himself at last.

He was looking forward to picking up the first load next Saturday. A couple of weeks earlier he had submitted his resignation from his position as a personnel officer at Standard Telephones and Cables (better known as STC) and was confident he would soon be making good money.

It was March 1946, only six months after the end of World War Two, and Sydney was full of young men recently discharged from the forces. Cashed up with their deferred pay, they were now looking for a new job or a business idea. Ken had talked to Ray Miners, a relative who had a truck and was making money with the transport and sale of timber fence palings. Ray said they could be bought at a timber mill at Wyong, about 100 miles north of Sydney for threepence each. House owners in the outer suburbs had not been able to get fence palings during the war and were now happy to pay sixpence each. Ken found that Ray, with no education or trade, was making twice as much as he was with his two university degrees. When Ken asked if he could get part of the action, Ray said he would need a truck and be able to drive it. To Ray's surprise, Ken said he would buy a truck and learn to drive it, so Ray promised to help Ken get started.

Ken had thought of an Army disposal truck, as they were available, but then decided against that because many of those trucks had a rough history. Ken was no mechanic and he wanted to give reliable service to his customers, so he decided a new truck would be safer with less problems. It was to be an International KS5, a five ton table top, imported from the USA, as International trucks were not made in Australia until 1951. Because they were in short supply it was necessary to get a permit to buy the truck and then wait a month for delivery.

The list price of the truck was £833. Ken paid a deposit of £272 from his own savings account, and then arranged hire purchase finance. The wartime fixed prices regulation still applied.

When the truck was nearly ready for delivery, Ken contacted Ray and told him he was all set to go to Wyong for the first load, only to find that the mill had closed down and was out of business. Ray had promised Ken it was a good opportunity, now the promise was broken before it started. Ken learnt the realities of business.

With this setback, Ken realised availability of work for the truck was the major consideration; so he asked STC if he could withdraw his resignation and keep his clerical job. That would give him time to rethink his position. He had a wife, two young children and a mortgage to support.

———————————

Kenneth William Thomas was a country boy, born in Harden New South Wales on 15th June 1913. He was the second-youngest of six children in the family of Arthur Picton Thomas and Elizabeth (nee McLeod). There were three girls: Alexandria, Julia and Jean. Ken's two brothers were Arthur and Ross.

Ken's paternal grandparents, John and Julia Thomas, had come from Builth Wells in Wales. They arrived in Australia on board the 'Chimborazo' on 10th October 1881, with their three older children, William, Albert and Isabella. The fourth child, born in 1883, was Ken's father, Arthur Picton Thomas, who became better known as Gart. There was a fifth child, Julia Margaret, nine years younger than Gart.

John was a stonemason, and moved the family to Harden to make head-stones. The funeral Director died so John took over the business. There was a need as the nearest undertaker was at Young, about 50km away; a long distance before motor transport. On 30th April 1897 John died at age 49 with a cerebral tumour. Then his second son, Albert, helped Julia run the business for a couple of years.

Gart was only 16 when he took over from Albert, and then Julia relied on Gart to lead the funeral processions from the church to the cemetery.

A funeral in a country town was an important event. The deceased would be known to all the locals, so the shopkeepers would close their doors. Customers and staff would assemble on the footpath to show their respect as the funeral went past. From all the Murrumburrah and Harden churches a funeral went down Albury Street, the main street, then up the Demondrille Hill to the cemetery, a journey of about a kilometre.

Gart managed the whole proceedings with flawless solemnity. He bor-rowed two beautiful black horses from a local man to pull the hearse.

Top: *The village of Builth, Wales, home of Ken's grandparents before migrating to Australia.*
Bottom: *A horse-drawn hearse of the late 19th century.*

Tall and dignified, dressed in a frock coat and a stove pipe hat, Gart caught the attention and interest of Elizabeth McLeod, daughter of a local farming family.

When the funeral business was sold in 1902, Gart tried several jobs before becoming a railwayman. That meant starting as a coal shoveler, then becoming a fireman, before getting his driver's ticket. Gart was good at the physical part, but his short time at school meant he had a struggle with the arithmetic and written tests. The examiner, realising the problem, told him to take a break for a while, then said to older brother, Edwin, known as Ned, who was the scholar, "Gart is having a problem, and while he has lunch I left his paper in the room, but forgot to lock it." So in due course Gart qualified as a driver and was able to wear the bowler hat and weskit, the insignia of a steam-engine driver.

Arthur Picton Thomas (Gart).
Born 7/10/1882 at Picton,
died 1965 at Chatswood.

In later years, Ken was very proud that his father had been a train driver. For a while Gart Thomas had Ben Chifley as his fireman. Ken used to boast, "My father was Ben Chifley's boss, and when they stopped working Ben had been Prime Minister, and my father an engine driver."

Harden—and its twin town Murrumburrah was a railway junction on the Sydney to Melbourne line with a branch line to Young, Cowra and Blayney.

Clockwise from left: 1. Presbyterian Church, now Uniting, Harden. 2. Murrumburrah Primary School in Ken's time. 3. Harden railway station.

This was the Demondrille branch; it was a connection between the southern and western NSW lines. Murrumburrah-Harden had a population of about 2000 people. The district was and still is a grain and sheep farming area, on the New South Wales south-west slopes, 360km from Sydney.

Ken's maternal grandfather, Rhody McLeod, was a Scot, born in 1838 on the Isle of Skye. He came at age 12 with his family to Australia. They went to the south-west slopes and became early pioneers of the Cullinga district. In 1870 Rhody married Elizabeth Lawford at Young. Together they established a farm, cleared and tilled virgin land, grew crops, tended sheep, and

ONE TOWN WITH TWO NAMES

Murrumburrah-Harden is a bit of a mystery to visitors. Why have two names, when there is only one town? The answer is that it is the New South Wales Railways who were responsible for that.

Murrumburrah was the name of a sheep station, and the first business was an inn which opened in the 1850s. The village became a town and in 1879 the Great Southern railway line from Goulburn reached it and Murrumburrah railway station was built.

There was a problem: the cold nights and icy winter weather made the rails very slippery, and trains had difficulty in getting traction after stopping at the station.

Another station was built on the hill, about a mile north, and it was called Harden. The railway employees wanted to live close by, and hotels were needed for travellers and thirsty railway men, so the town of Harden grew.

In the 20th century the two towns grew and merged, and there is no physical line between them. Both names are used. For example, the one high school, quite close to Harden railway station, is the Murrumburrah High School.

overcame loneliness and hardship. The nearest doctor was at Young, and the railway line then terminated at Goulburn.

Rhody planted wheat in the biblical way, with a sheet tied around his neck and held with his left hand and throwing the seed over the ground with the right hand. The children followed to chase the birds away and cover the seed. The family was eight girls and two boys.

One of these girls was also named Elizabeth, and it was she who had set her eye on Gart as he led the funeral processions. They married in 1904.

Ken described his grandfather Rhody as a devout Presbyterian, hard working and canny, but he could not read or write, signing with his mark 'X'. His grand-daughter Emily, who was raised by her grandparents after her mother died, would read Zane Gray stories to him.

Ken would later write in glowing terms about his mother, who also received very little schooling.

"Coming from such circumstances, mother had the good sense to comprehend that education was the greatest privilege on earth. Her own lack of schooling inevitably produced an exaggerated respect for educated people, especially parsons. Her speech was immaculate, no doubt from listening to the two educated men she knew, Dr Heggaton, and Rev. Benjamin Evans of the Presbyterian Church. I believe she never read a book or saw a film."

Before she married, Ken's mother Elizabeth was a champion horsewoman, and won prizes at the local shows. She had a skirted riding habit to ride side saddle, and with a straight back, a firm seat and a natural style was a favourite local equestrienne.

Growing up in a modest working man's house, meeting his father's rail worker mates, exposed Ken to an understanding of people that would serve him well in later years when dealing and working with employees. It also gave him an understanding of, and a respect for, the railways that would prove very important in later years. To his dying day he was passionate about the advantages of rail transport.

Ken's mother managed the family. Gart handed over his wages, and the quietly spoken Elizabeth ran the household and saw to the education of the children.

Ken loved the freedom and adventure of a boy's life in a country town. Billy carts, climbing trees, wrestling, and barefooted chasing the cows through the frost before milking them, were the norm. Then there was rabbiting. Ken's elder brother Arthur and his mate carried the guns. Ken, the youngest, had to pick up and carry the dead 'uns. One day after a hunt, they were in the bedroom, cleaning a rifle with a faulty mechanism. A stray bullet went off; it missed Ken's head by an inch. The plaster wall was damaged, but some chewing gum repaired the hole. Fortunately Mum was out, so she never found out.

Ken told the 'Harden Spectacular' story for the rest of his life. Before sewerage and septic tanks, every house had an outside 'dunny'. There was a can which had to be collected and taken away by the 'dunny man'.

The dunny cart was a double-decker, two horse-drawn and the run was so well known by the horses that the dunny man let them move along the street as he collected the cans. In Ken's words:

"One day something had frightened the horses, and they took off. The cart bolted down the main street of Harden and into Clarke Street, where we lived. The horses

took the corner too fast; the cart had sliding doors, so as it lurched and swayed each slide opened doors and allowed more full cans to fall out. As they hit the road the lids fell off and the load went everywhere. The horses broke their harness and took off."

Sunday School was a definite must every week. Ken won many book prizes that he treasured. He called them 'beaut books'. He topped the state for Scripture, and later in life said the main requirement of the exam was to know the answers to 28 questions in the Shorter Catechism. The first one particularly appealed to him and became an objective for life.

Question: What is the chief end of man?

Answer: Mans' chief end is to glorify God and enjoy him forever.

Ken wrote, many years later, that "substituting Life, or Nature, for God, I am hooked on those eleven words."

For years he remembered and quoted this philosophy to others. Enjoyment of life and human happiness was his constant desire. For all his life he had a big raucous laugh and was always the centre of the party.

Something else Ken learned from his boyhood was the 'Christian work ethic' and a burning desire to succeed.

Ken's happy years in Harden-Murrumburrah branded him for life as a country boy. Love of the bush remained with him until the day he died.

It can well be said: *"You can take the boy out of the country, but you cannot take the country out of the boy."*

UPSETTING MRS COLE

In Ken's words:

"The dunnies were all located next to the back fence of each house. There was a flap door opening onto the lane, so the can could be slid out, loaded onto the double-decker cart, and be replaced with another can, empty and freshly tarred.

"Now Mrs Cole had the misfortune to live near the corner of the lane. She would emerge from the kitchen, promenade down the back, close the door and ascend the throne. We kids would be in the lane and silently open the flap door, poke some sticks up to tickle her bum. Shrieks of 'Snakes!' Hasty pulling up of drawers. By the time she emerged we were around the corner and gone."

"MY MOTHER HAD THE GOOD SENSE TO
BELIEVE THAT EDUCATION IS THE GREATEST
PRIVILEGE ON EARTH."

—*KEN THOMAS*

CHAPTER 2

THE PREPARATION YEARS

Ken's education was a paramount concern for his mother. Elizabeth realised that secondary schools available in Sydney offered better opportunities for him.

In 1924, when Ken was 11, Gart arranged a transfer to the Clyde railway depot, in western Sydney, where he would drive steam engines on the suburban services. For a while the family lived at Camperdown and then moved to Glebe, both inner suburbs.

Ken had a very good reference from the headmaster at Murrumburrah Primary School, who had suggested he go to Fort Street Boys High, one of the best Sydney schools. However, this was a selective school and an entrance exam was needed; so the headmaster warned it would be unlikely that Ken would be able to get in. The Thomas family were not deterred. They went to Fort Street and met the headmaster there, 'Dags' Kilgour, with a starched butterfly collar and a stern countenance. He said it was too late; notice of some months had to be given, an exam had to be passed, and anyway the

Fort Street Boys High School.

school was full. However, he liked country boys, so he interviewed Ken. Mr Kilgour was so impressed that he offered to fit him into the school.

While living at Glebe, Ken commenced his transport career with a billy cart delivery service of firewood. Down on Blackwattle Bay was the yard of the timber merchant, George Hudson. Ken and a mate would load up with timber offcuts and deliver to the locals for four shillings a load.

EARLY YEARS

Andrew, Gavin and Anne Thomas in North Queensland. Probably in 1969

Ken Thomas, a boy at heart in his favourite environment—the bush.

In the early 1950's, the unsealed road across the Nullabor was very rough. Ken directed that all trucks had to be piggybacked to Western Australia.

Top: Unloading in Brisbane c1958. NSW rail trucks had to be unloaded where there was a standard guage siding.

Bottom: NQX (North Queensland Express) trucks had a different livery. They operated from Sydney and Melbourne to North Queensland centres.

TNT built their own gantry cranes at rail yards, for the handling of containers.

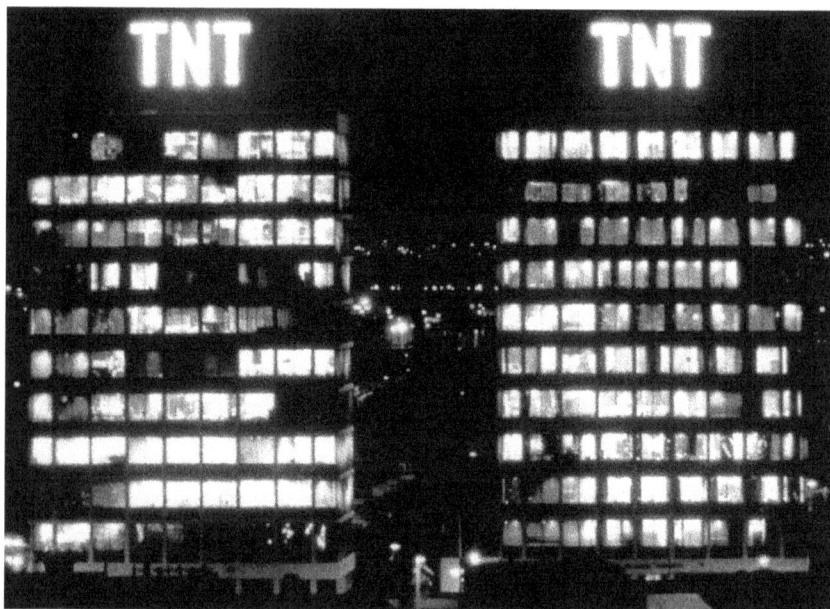

Top: TNT Courier Girls.

Bottom: TNT Towers at Redfern, Sydney.

Top: A TNT train. A complete train of TNT freight, a daily occurrence between Sydney and Melbourne from 1970. This train, in 1995 was running from Adelaide to Melbourne.

Bottom: A rare sight. An electric locomotive hauls a TNT train near Wyong, NSW in February 1989. The train would have originated in Brisbane, the locomotive attached at Broadmeadow.

These two diesel locomotives were some of the first introduced in Australia in 1952. Now they are maintained and run in NSW by the Rail Transport Museum.

FORT STREET
HIGH SCHOOL

Ken was indeed fortunate in being able to enrol at Fort Street. The school has a very proud history with a good reputation and record.

The school is the oldest selective high school in NSW, founded in 1849 at Observatory Hill, an area near the southern approach to the Sydney Harbour Bridge.

In 1916 the boys' section was moved to Taverner's Hill at Petersham, where Ken went. Since then the school has become co-educational.

There are some well known names amongst the Old Boys, including Garfield Barwick and Alan Walker, both of whom would later cross paths with Ken.

Ken later wrote: "I was the operations manager as well as being in charge of marketing. How I managed to flog it beats me, because the old ducks would have to axe it into narrower lengths, then cut it across the grain to fit into their stoves. I was the front man because I was a pretty little soft brown-eyed fella and could talk 'proper'. We sold a lot of loads but I don't remember getting any repeat orders."

The family bought a house at 90 Park Road, Auburn. This became Ken's home until he married. From there Gart could walk to work. In 1926 the first electric trains started running in Sydney and Gart wanted to move up to driving the new trains but he failed the exam. No big brother to help this time.

Gart found that living in Sydney was not to his liking. He missed his long standing railway mates at Harden; he had failed in his attempt to drive electric trains and he was marooned politically. All his life Gart supported the Nationalist Party. The Nationalists were the conservative, right wing opposition to Labor; they later became the Liberal Party. During the 1917 railway strike Gart was declared a scab because he continued working. He got into a fight at Goulburn because of his politics. So living and working in Sydney was for the family, not him.

About this time Ken's mother, Elizabeth, won £5 in a competition. That was a lot of money, about a man's weekly wage, and she asked Ken what would he like her to buy for him. Ken selected a second-hand book, Websters Dictionary & Reference Book, a huge publication of about 3000 pages. It contained an encyclopedia, history and geography material. This book was precious to Ken then and for the rest of his life. He kept it in the dining room of his home and used it to settle many family meal-time arguments. The book is now a treasured possession of Rhody, Ken's eldest son. Not many teenagers would have made such a selection.

Ken sat for the Intermediate Certificate in 1928. In those days for most people, the Intermediate after three years of high school was the culmination of their education, so it was important. Ken passed in seven subjects: A in Maths I, Latin and History, and B in English, Maths II, French and Science. A good result. However, it was not enough for university entrance. That would need two more years at high school, and the family could not afford that.

At age 15, Ken left school and found a job at the State Savings Bank as a junior, and before long he graduated to a teller. That was an important position, in those days only open to males. The Depression was being felt, and Ken met unemployed people who were desperate to withdraw their savings from the bank. Although the bank was owned by the New South Wales Government it was not liquid enough to pay them all. The customers were left to sell their bank books for a fraction of the bank balance. They assigned away money they could ill afford to lose. This was legal and advertisements were in the papers for sale of bank books for as little as 12/6 in the pound. At that price people lost 37.5% of their savings. The State Savings Bank was later taken over by the Federal Government-owned Commonwealth Bank.

Living in Auburn, the Thomas family were in the electorate of Jack Lang, then Labor leader in the State Parliament. Lang, known widely as 'The Big Fella' was a real estate agent with an office in the main street near the railway station. Beside the office, he had a platform built so that he could address his constituents. Ken was one of those who stopped, on the way to and from the train, to hear what Lang had to say.

The Depression was a demoralising time. One out of three working men were without a job. Sir Bertram Stevens, the Nationalist Leader, had said that if Lang was elected there would be a run on the State Bank. Lang won the election on

In Rockhampton the railway line goes down a major residential street. Being a train lover, Ken had a good view of the many trains taking wartime supplies north.

30th May 1925 and became Premier. Later, there was a run, despite the fact that the bank was guaranteed by the government. Labor advocated increased government spending, while the Nationalists wanted to cut spending. This policy so disgusted Ken that from then on he disliked the Conservatives, whether Nationalists, or later the UAP (United Australia Party) or Liberals. However, he wrote that he never joined the Labor Party.

History has proved that Ken and Jack Lang were right. In times of Depression, when jobs are scarce, and money is tight, government spending has the effect of stimulating employment and the economy. That was a lesson Australia learnt the hard way in the 1930s.

Ken realised he had to improve his education. A university degree became his aim. Firstly he had to go to Sydney Technical College to do the extra high school work for matriculation. He completed that work in 1932. From there, he went to Sydney University to gain an Arts degree. He studied Philosophy, Psychology, Latin and Greek. He graduated in 1935, aged 22. Then, deciding he wanted more, Ken went on to gain an Economics degree. This was all done at night and he kept a job while he studied.

One result of the university experience was that Ken questioned his religious training and beliefs. From being a committed Christian, Ken became an atheist. For the rest of his life he followed Christian principles but denied being a Christian; and he was not afraid to make his beliefs known. This was later to prove very expensive for him.

In the days before calculators, a bank teller had to be quick and accurate with figures. Ken gave himself practice by adding up a column of telephone numbers in the phone book. The bank closed at 3pm, and the tellers were free to go when they had balanced their day's work; so Ken kept on top, by balancing at morning tea time and again at lunch time. This made it quick and easy for him to finalise at 3pm and be off to do some study.

Having graduated with his two degrees Ken decided after seven years to move on from the bank. He tried teaching, with a year at Trinity Grammar, a leading private school then at Strathfield, but he found that teaching was not for him. Even so, he must have been an effective teacher as 76 years later one of his primary school pupils, David Hull, a retired doctor, had happy memories of Ken as his teacher, and was able to describe the car Ken drove.

After a year at Trinity Grammar, Ken's love for the country prevailed and he went to Dalby in Queensland for a few months, but he did not stay long and returned to Sydney.

In the 1930s jobs were not easy to get but Ken had several. He became a salesman and found he had a natural skill for sales work. He was able to see opportunities and that would become very important in later life. He had a year as a van salesman for Lever Bros (Unilever) and then time as a salesman for the petrol company, Ampol.

Ken found that a secretary at Lever Bros was Anne McKinnon, a girl he had first met at university. In due course they became engaged and were married in St Peter's Presbyterian Church at North Sydney on 23rd December 1939.

When war broke out in 1939, Ken decided he did not want to join the armed services. But he did want to make a contribution to the war effort; so he volunteered to the Manpower Commission for a position as a personnel officer with the Department of Labour and National Service. He was posted to Melbourne to work as a personnel officer at the Maribyrnong munitions factory. The family lived in a rented house in Essendon. Ken was later to write that another woman in Essendon had observed, "Mrs Thomas is not stuck up, but she does talk proper."

In 1942 when the war was severely threatening Australia, Ken decided to volunteer for the Air Force. However he was advised that his job was essential to the war effort and his offer was rejected. To challenge his skills as a personnel officer, Ken was sent to the Rockhampton meatworks in 1944.

The supply of food was an important part of the war effort and the William Angliss cattle abattoir supplied large quantities of beef. Rockhampton was above the Brisbane line, and Ken did not want to risk his family's security, so Annie and young daughter Elizabeth remained in Melbourne. While there, their second child, Rhody, was born. The Brisbane line marked the part of Australia considered most at risk if the Japanese invaded and occupied

Australia. That did not happen, but Ken did make a big impression on the meatworkers; one of them wrote a poem:

TROPICAL WELFARE

(A saga of the meatworks)

It was somewhere up near Capricorn, beyond the Brisbane line.
Where the bullocks were complaining of the heat,
And the bullock driving gentry too were feeling far from fine,
Not knowing that they were soon to have a treat.

When the monsoons hit the tropics then the niggers die like flies.
And beer goes up to three and six a pot.
Then the white man bears his burden as with bleary blood shot eyes
he steels his soul to bear his awful lot.

In a meatworks in the jungle where the tree tops graze the skies,
and strange creeping crawling creatures lie in wait,
where the absentee percentage is for ever on the rise
as the callous cattle canners dice with fate.

In a shanty town in Shanty Town beside the Coral Sea
there's a fan tan school that never closes down,
and the bland celestial owner rubs his hands to show his glee,
every time his takings rise by half a crown.

And his pretty slant eyed daughter gliding softly in and out,
makes the place more attractive to the boys.
She serves them with fire water every time the gamblers shout,
and doesn't seem to mind the glare and noise.

To this jungle hell came Thomas, better known as kindly Ken,
and his smiling face lit up the tropic murk,
as he set out on a programme to reform his fellow men,
who had formed a rather strong dislike for work.

First he got them all alarm clocks for an early morning start,
which was quite a new departure in their lives.
Then he made them give up gambling, this was quite the hardest part,
But they could now take their wages to their wives.

And the gambling den proprietor grew thin and old and grey,
lack of customers soon bowed him down in grief,
But our Kenneth's welfare programme roped him in that very day,
sticking labels on the tins of bully beef.

And his daughter's on the payroll at the meat works by the creek,
she was known to all the world as Shanghai Sue,
As a typist she has dignity at four pound ten per week,
and is called by all respectfully—Miss Lou.

Now the meat production programme it has reached an all time high,
the absence problem now is at an end,
for the workers all are happy—the millennium is nigh,
because they know that kindly Kenneth is their friend.

After the war was won, Ken carefully considered his position. He remembered well the advice of his grandfather, the canny Scot Rhody Mcleod, to be self-employed to gain financial security. With experience from the variety of work he had done and the conditions in the post-war period, he saw transport as being a way to do something for himself, and he could raise the capital to do it.

Ken had not driven a truck, and he had no passion for them. Transport just made economic sense to him. This was where Ken was different. Most road transport operators, truckies, have diesel fuel in their blood; their music is a throbbing engine, and behind the wheel they are in heaven. But Ken was not like that. He was a man with brains. While others with two university degrees might find it below their dignity to do so, Ken was prepared to work beside and with the blue collar men.

That way would prove to be successful.

"DO NOT RESIST CHANGE,
BECAUSE CHANGE IS VITALITY."

—*KEN THOMAS*

FINDING HIS FEET

In 1946, Ken was devastated. He had paid the deposit and organised the finance for his new truck, and was fully committed.

"What now?" he asked himself.

The plan to bring fence palings from Wyong was in tatters and there was no other source of income in view. Ray had let him down.

Ken rethought his position. His salary as a personnel officer at STC was £12 a week, and that was more than a driver's wages. STC had agreed to him withdrawing his resignation, so he could stay. This guaranteed him enough to support the family until the truck was working profitably. If he hired a driver, the truck would have to make enough to pay a driver and the loan repayments.

Ken looked for a driver, and located Frank Legge still wearing his RAAF uniform. Ken had no office of course, so he arranged to meet Frank on the footpath for the interview outside the *Sydney Morning Herald* office in O'Connell Street.

On 18th March 1946, the truck was registered, and Frank was learning to drive it. Ken had been scouting around looking for carrying work, and K.W.Thomas was in the transport business.

One of the first jobs was the transport of lavatory pans from Malley's destined for Wollongong. They had to go by rail from Darling Harbour, because of the road tax imposed by the State Government. This was applicable when road transport carried freight that could have gone by rail. So K.W.Thomas had the job of carting the pans to Darling Harbour.

Ken took some time off work to assist Frank and learn the trade. The truck was loaded before they realised they had only very thick rope in a long length. That was most inappropriate to hold the pans on the truck. It did have gate sides, but a light rope was needed. So they had to rectify that problem first. The rate agreed on was 10/6 per ton (about $1.05). The load, 7ft high and 14ft long, weighed only two and a half tons. There was a delay at Darling Harbour; to find their way round and wait for a rail truck meant the job took a whole day. The revenue was equivalent to $2.65. Fortunately Malley's Transport Manager understood the problem and agreed to pay on a time basis. It was a big learning experience for Ken and Frank.

An early job was a truck-load of empty bottles that fell off in Bridge Street in the city. Ken had to quickly buy a broom and sweep up a mountain of broken glass.

At weekends Ken would do some work by himself. He made trips to Berrima about 150km away, to collect bags of cement. There was no time wasted: he was able to leave Sydney late on Friday afternoon, get to Berrima, load eight tons of cement in bags, and be home by 4am for a quick sleep before delivering to hardware shops on Saturday morning. Hard work for a truck rated for a five ton load. No fork lifts of course, so in an eight-ton load there were 124 bags to be lifted and carried by a "little fellow" all of 5'6."

Another weekend earner was the collection and delivery of garden soil on Sundays. Ken recruited a friend to help, and very early in the morning they went to the Lane Cove Park. Ken paid the caretaker four shillings (40 cents) 'to go for a walk' while they loaded. All by shovel, no mechanical equipment in those days. The soil was rich and dark and looked good. An advertisement in the *Sydney Morning Herald* cost 16 and sixpence, and said "garden soil, rich in humus in 1 to 6 ton lots." The problem turned out to be that instead of fertilising lawns, it withered them and killed all the customer's plants. They later found that the soil was contaminated with chemicals from factories in the area. So Ken had to find another source of soil and then travel much further, out to Liverpool, to get it.

An early success was a contract with Farmer & Co (later Myer) to deliver purchases to customers' homes. In the days before there was a car in every household, home deliveries were an important service.

While Ken was out working, Annie was at home with the children; she took the phone messages about jobs and passed them on to Ken or the driver.

Ken kept some records about the expenditure in that initial period. A week's wages to Frank was £6/15/0. Then Ken paid a bonus of 15 shillings, plus 10% of the previous week's profit to Frank.

While these costs were significant to Ken at the time, they look paltry in the 21st century.

Petrol, he wrote, was 31.5 pence per gallon which is equivalent to seven cents per litre. A weighbridge ticket cost nine pence, and a sign writer charged £1/5/0 to put K W THOMAS, CARRIER on the truck's door.

At 30th June 1946, Ken calculated that his net income for the first 15 weeks of being in business was £60/16/0. All that work for £4 per week, and when depreciation was allowed for, there was no profit.

Ken found it all very tough going, and sang to himself the negro ballad:

> *Sixteen tons and what do you get*
> *Another day over and deeper in debt.*
> *St Peter don't call me because I can't go,*
> *I owe my soul to the company store.*

Ken really considered getting out before he got into bigger problems, but he knew he would lose money selling the truck. He recalled Toynbee writing "without tension there is no creation."

Then he thought of other successful businesses that had made a scrounging start, so he kept going.

Before he had taken delivery of the truck, Ken had met the Secretary of the NSW Master Carrier's Association, Jack Beecham, and discussed his prospects.

The Master Carriers' Association was the trade group for the Road Transport Industry, and they had for many years set the rates that members were required to charge. Price fixing with competitors was then a normal business practice.

Jack told Ken that the industry was full of young men trying to make a living and they were all finding it hard going, so suggested Ken not go ahead with his plan to enter the industry.

While Ken rejected the advice, the call paid off. A few months later Jack Beecham was asked by a Melbourne company, Pizzey Pty Ltd, for the name of a reliable carrier to take a load from Melbourne to Sydney. The company was in the hides and leather business, and hides treated in Melbourne were needed in a hurry at the Sydney plant. Hides are smelly and not easy to handle so Pizzey would pay a good price. Ken arranged for the truck to take eight tons of cement from the cement works at Kandos to Melbourne. The town of Kandos is about 200 km west of Sydney. Cement from the factory normally went by rail, but there was a rail strike, so the road tax was temporarily lifted. There was no bitumen road to Kandos so it was a rough trip for Frank.

The normal rail transit time between Kandos and Melbourne was 10 to 12 days, but Frank was able to do the trip much quicker. All the arrangements Ken had made went very well, and what seemed to be a formidable feat was a breeze. When Ken looked at the figures he thought it was too good to be true.

So interstate carrying seemed to be the way to go. However, there were problems; Ken was not at all sure that interstate carrying could be the basis for a successful business.

The railways had industrial problems, their service was slow, inefficient, and made worse by the change of gauge at Albury. Businesses had need of a reliable transport service, but if they used road transport they were obliged to pay the road tax.

In August 1946 the rail problem was so bad that the NSW Government temporarily lifted all restrictions on road transport. No road tax would be payable, and trucks could carry freight to any part of the state, but owners would have to obtain a permit at the cost of one shilling.

There were only a few trucks suitable for long distance haulage, and the need for trucks was so great there was talk of bringing in the Army to assist. If extra trucks could be found, the industry knew that the government would reimpose the restrictions as soon as they could; the extra trucks would lie idle, and the drivers would have to be laid off. Even if the restrictions were lifted by the New South Wales Government, other states might not do the same so the restrictions would be in place for the part of the journey in another state. To add to the bureaucratic nightmare, petrol rationing, which was imposed during the war, still applied and petrol coupons were sometimes not available. So what had at first seemed to be a golden opportunity, had problems and traps for a young struggling business.

There was another worry too. The Chifley Labor Federal Government was in power with a socialism policy. The government wanted to nationalise the banks, and there was talk of also nationalising road transport. In 1947 the United Kingdom Parliament decided that all road transport was to be government owned. The thought that this could also happen in Australia had a demoralising effect on the Australian transport industry.

There were some goods the railways did not like to handle for various reasons. One of these was carbon black, a fine black powder that was packed in paper bags. Sometimes the bags leaked or broke and made a real mess. The extra handling of these bags by rail transport led to more damage so the railways banned them, and the road tax did not apply. So the trick of the trade was to load something heavy, such as metal ingots, on the floor of the truck, and then cover them with bags of carbon black. When the truck was stopped for an inspection the Inspector had no desire to move the carbon black, so the whole load was passed as tax free, when tax should have been paid on the ingots.

Another early job was a request to take a boiler to Melbourne. The boiler was larger than the railways wanted to carry, and there was no ship available so Ken's quote was large enough to allow a return empty to Sydney. Ken went too, as offsider for Frank. Nearing Melbourne, they had a fire when the truck overheated, so Ken used his coat to beat it out. After unloading, they looked for a return load, and found there was plenty of freight available and a good price could be charged.

Ken was passionate about building a reputation for service and as his repu-tation grew so did the business. As extra trucks were needed Ken bought some cheap war surplus vehicles, and before long he had three tabletops and a small 18-foot semitrailer all working. Managing and finding work for them was quite a job, so in 1948 Ken decided that he would leave the 'day job' he then had, as Survey Officer with the Cumberland County Council, to manage his business. This gave him more time to look for new customers.

Business premises were needed too. Until then the business was run from his home, and there was no yard for the trucks. Something had to be done.

In 1948 a friend told Ken about Campbell and Landers Pty Ltd. This was a small carrying firm with a freehold depot at 100 Beattie St, Balmain, and it was on the market. The company had been established in 1938, there were some vehicles and customers, and best all was the depot. It was in a good position; Balmain was an inner industrial suburb of Sydney, there was an old weatherboard house and an adjacent two-storey building. There was plenty of space for the handling and loading of freight and a workshop for vehicle repairs. Ken decided to buy the whole company. This became his first takeover.

One day a woman who owned a truck, a war surplus vehicle, offered to do overflow work as a subcontractor. This was a new concept to Ken. Later it proved a good way to have extra trucks at no capital costs. It became possible to tie the subbie in, by paying for his/her truck to have K.W Thomas colours to increase the exposure. This practice became widely used and an important feature in the growth of the Australian Transport Industry.

The expansion meant that extra management was needed.

When he was at Cumberland County Council, Ken had made friends with another employee there, Geoff Hammond. Geoff was born in Sydney on 3rd June 1921, and had served in the 2/5 Independent Company of the Army in Papua New Guinea during the War. While in the Army he had met Lillian Wall, and they married in 1947. They lived in a flat at Crows Nest, with their first child, Christine, born in 1948.

After his Army discharge Geoff went to Sydney University and graduated with an Economics degree, with First Class Honours in 1949.

As a workmate, Geoff had helped Ken with his financial records from the early days; he learnt a lot about the business and he could see its future potential. It was only natural that when the business needed a full time accountant, Ken offered Geoff the job. Geoff designed an accounting system that was simple, accurate and quick. Ken was always one to want a weekly report on the financial situation. He knew that was an important tool in any business. It was up to Geoff, as the 'figures man' to prepare these reports.

The management team in 1950. From left: Ken Smith, Sydney Manager; Bill Martin, Adelaide Manager; Geoff Hammond, Group Accountant; Henrietta Searle, Clerk; Ken Thomas, Governing Director; Max Arnetts, Melbourne Manager.

There was a need for an Operations Manager to manage things each day to allow Ken the time to go out to sell the services.

Two doors down from the Thomas household at Castlecrag lived the Smith family: Ken and Joan with three children. Ken Smith had a distinguished war record in the RAAF; he had risen to the rank of Flight Lieutenant, as he specialised in navigation and then the calibration of radar.

After his demobilisation in 1946, Ken Smith had re-joined his father in the grocery business, which was prospering. A block of land at 11 The Bastion, Castlecrag, was bought, a builder engaged, and the family moved in to their new house. They loved the place and got to know the neighbours. When Ken Smith's father asked Ken and family to move to Melbourne, to open a branch of the grocery business there, they were not happy. Joan Smith told her friend Anne Thomas, and when Ken Thomas heard the news, he saw the opportunity to recruit Ken Smith. Ken Smith became the Operations Manager of K.W.Thomas.

The three men, Ken Thomas, Geoff Hammond and Ken Smith, fitted in together very well and they complemented each other to make a team. They made a habit of a 7am. meeting in the office every day when they would discuss problems and set the policy of the business.

In February 1948, Ken Thomas was instrumental in the formation of the Long Distance Road Transport Association (LDRTA). Ken declined the presidency as he thought a more independent and non-competitor, in the form of Vince Rowe, would be a wise choice. Ken was elected vice-president, and a trustee.

The objectives of the LDRTA were to discuss with the New South Wales Minister of Transport, and the Commissioner of Transport, the anomalies in road tax and the regulations in force.

There was a plan to have a 'Freight Exchange' where members could dispose of or pick up excess loadings and hire trucks and drivers to each other. A major objective was to establish some freight rates so that members did not undercut each other.

The members discussed the concept of no night driving, and the payment of sufficient money to the drivers to allow them proper meals and accommodation en route. It was agreed that a reasonable time for a Sydney-Melbourne trip was two and a half days.

A major objective of the LDRTA was to have the road tax rate changed to a price per ton of cargo for a particular run. The rate in force was a rate per ton mile, but the tare weight of the truck was included, even if it was a part load or travelling empty. The Association told the New South Wales Government that they accepted the need for some control and tax, but a fairer system would result in in a better compliance and cooperation by the industry. That concept was never accepted by the government.

Petrol rationing was also on the agenda, and some progress was made when there was a Federal Government guarantee that there would be petrol coupons available when a trip permit was issued. Petrol rationing was in place until 1950, and was then lifted following an election promise made by Robert Menzies in the 1949 federal election campaign.

When Ken bought the Campbell and Landers property and business it included the company structure of Campbell and Landers Pty Ltd. Ken changed the company name to Kragteam Pty Ltd. K. W. Thomas Transport Co was owned by Kragstream, and Ken and his family owned all the shares in the company.

In 1951 a new company was formed; K.W.Thomas Transport Pty Ltd then owned the transport business. Ken wanted to recognise the participation and dedication of Geoff Hammond and Ken Smith so they were each offered a directorship and one-third of the shares. As they had insufficient money to buy them, there was provision for them to pay by instalments over three years. The interest on the loan was 8.5%.

One of the early developments was the designing of a freight note. This was a simple document, filled in by the consignor, with details of the cargo and its destination. There was provision for the insertion of the charges by the carrier, and a copy of the document went to the party responsible as an invoice for paying the bill.

This sounds so simple now, but it was something not previously done in the transport industry. Until that time there would be a charge for picking up the goods to be despatched by rail or sea, another account for the main haul, and a third for the delivery at destination. Other transport companies later followed, but K.W. Thomas Transport Pty Ltd led the way with this improvement.

The next step was the establishment of interstate branches. It was very obvious that the first had to be in Melbourne, so Max Annetts was despatched from Sydney to open that. There was of course a need for transport to other states as well as Victoria.

So the decision was made to cover Australia with a branch in each state. A Sydney company would like to have its favoured carrier take all they had to go interstate. Naturally K.W. Thomas wanted to handle it all. Then when a truck had unloaded at the destination city a back load was needed. With a local branch of the company, that would be arranged.

Each state manager was appointed to organise a branch and build up a local team to make the network effective. Naturally they had to find new business as well, as each branch was measured as a cost and revenue centre. These capital city branches had all been set up by the early 1950s.

Sometimes accidents happen.

Typical was the experience of Bill Martin. After discharge from his Army service at the end of the war, Bill found it hard to get a job, until he was employed as "a general help round the place for a very small transport company."

In 1950 he joined Ken Thomas, who then had 18 employees. Bill started as the loading supervisor, then a foreman. In February 1951 he, and Cec Van de Velde were sent by Ken to open a branch in Adelaide. Bill went on to a long and successful career with TNT. Looking back, Bill said, "to work for Ken Thomas in the early days, you had to be able to lift half a ton in one hand and write a manifest with the other."

In 1953 Geoff Hammond was asked by Ken to go to Melbourne and be responsible for the southern states. All the branch managers in Victoria,

South Australia, Tasmania and Western Australia would report to Geoff as a director of the company. Geoff did that very successfully and remained in that position until 1967.

The Hammond family lived in Beaumaris, a suburb of Melbourne, and Geoff was close enough to the water to be a regular sailor. He decided to build his own yacht, which he completed in 1964, with the dream of sailing the world.

One of Geoff's early triumphs in Melbourne was winning the Myer business. He convinced Myer that they should tell all their suppliers that K.W. Thomas was the carrier to transport all the merchandise for Myer to Melbourne. This was a real bonus as it told the business world that Myer were using K.W. Thomas, so they must be a good carrier. The triumph nearly ended in tears, as the first truck with Myer goods had an accident on the way down and damaged the load. Geoff had to hot foot it into the store and convince the sceptical managers that sometimes accidents happen, but not often. Geoff saved the day, and kept the account.

The establishment of branches was one of the triumphs of Ken Thomas. He had started running trucks interstate very early after the war, when few if any other carriers were doing that. The competitors did not have branches in each state. They all appointed agents to work with in other places, with varying degrees of effectiveness. The biggest transport companies at that time, Mayne Nickless, F.H. Stephens, Brambles, and Rudders, did not have branches in each state until the late 1950s, or even into the 1960s.

The other companies did little interstate transport by road. Although they had a long history, back to the 19th century for Mayne Nickless and F.H.Stephens, they operated as forwarders. They would collect cargo from a customer, then take it to a rail yard or wharf to be sent to the destination. Sometimes the agent

Mechanics and drivers at Balmain depot.

at the destination would collect at the rail depot or wharf and deliver. Ken Thomas pioneered the door-to-door concept that became standard within a few years. The service offered one carrier, one charge, and one company responsible to the customer. In many cases the customer had a choice about the method of transport that best suited.

This was the key to Ken's success.

Running a fleet of trucks had its worries for Ken Thomas, as the work was tough on the vehicles and that meant mechanical problems and needs.

Ken was no mechanic. Luckily in 1950 Ken met Arthur Bray. Arthur was employed by a garage at Gundagai, and he had been called out a number of times by Ken's drivers when they struck mechanical problems in the hilly areas of the Hume Highway on the road to Melbourne.

The first time Ken Thomas saw Arthur was about 3am one cold morning, after Ken had taken a crankshaft to his Inter KB7 truck broken down near Tarcutta. Ken found the truck and noticed two feet projecting from beneath the vehicle. Ken was impressed that somebody was so dedicated to get the truck going, to be working at that time of day, that he had a conversation with the feet and offered them, and the rest of the body, a job. A few weeks later the feet walked into Ken's office at Balmain and Arthur was put in charge of mechanical maintenance of the fleet.

A few months later Ken asked Arthur what they should do with the "crummy, hot potch fleet, as it is costly to run and needs a heap of off-the-shelf spare parts." Although he had started with a new truck, Ken had not resisted the low prices on some second-hand ex-Army trucks, as more trucks were needed. Now this was a problem.

Within a month Arthur had looked at the trucks then available; he had decided that the work justified new vehicles, and that they should standardise on one make: Leyland. Six new Leyland Beavers could be bought on time payment hire purchase finance, which meant the old trucks could be scrapped.

Ken agreed to this arrangement and was very pleased with the result. Those six new trucks were to give splendid service and became the backbone for the K.W. Thomas Pty Ltd road operations. They never broke down.

In fact trucks of this class were rare in the interstate operations of that time. Most of the other operators were battlers and in the 1950s were driving Commers, 180 Internationals and Bedfords. Most of them were restricted to a 12-ton load, as they pulled a single-axle semi-trailer. A few had bogie trailers, and there were even some table-tops. Vehicles were way under powered at a time when the hills were frequent and steep. The whole Hume Highway had one lane in each direction, so a regular and annoying experience for motorists was to crawl along behind a slow truck that was belching out clouds of black smoke and waiting for a chance to overtake.

Arthur Bray's services were so appreciated by Ken Thomas that he went on to take control of vehicles Australia-wide and organised maintenance teams in each capital city. This included responsibility for buying the vehicles, semi-trailers and other equipment.

Along the road, even the Hume Highway, the main Melbourne to Sydney route, things were difficult for the drivers. There were few places where it was possible to get a meal close to where it was safe to park a truck. Overnight accommodation was hard to find, particularly as uncertainty of arrival times made booking impossible. That meant many drivers had to sleep in or underneath their trucks; the idea of a sleeper cab was not thought of. Opening hours of the shops and service stations were for the convenience of the local people; long-distance travellers were then very few and far between.

Then there were the government regulations. In Victoria, trucks were not allowed on the road on Sundays, so there was a Saturday scramble to beat that, or a huge gathering of trucks in Albury waiting for a midnight take off to be ahead in the Monday morning race to Melbourne. New South Wales also had restrictions, and trucks had to wait at Picton on Sundays before an evening run into Sydney.

Above: The Tumbalong half way depot.

Right: Arthur Bray (far right) checks a truck engine block. In those days at Balmain, he frequently went to bed at 4am in a truck cabin, woke at 6am and had breakfast at a corner fish 'n' chip shop, and at 7am started work again.

As the number of trucks grew, the business people along the road saw the opportunities and began to cater for the truckies.

When they reached their destination cities, the drivers had to find the delivery points and then think about refuelling and finding a backload. That meant parking and security problems. Ken Thomas realised very early that a visiting driver needed a depot to head for, and the local people to be ready to help him get the services needed, including a load, and so be able to get rolling again as soon as possible.

To make things easier for the drivers, Ken bought a service station in Tumbalong in June 1950. This was about 14km south of Gundagai, near the famous Dog on The Tuckerbox, and about halfway between Sydney and Melbourne. Ken then asked Arthur and Ivy Prior to live there and manage the facility. Ivy was a friend of Ken's wife, Anne.

This gave the drivers a place to look forward to. Ivy would have a meal ready and a bed made; the trucks were refuelled and any minor truck repairs attended to. Arthur was to assist and then report their departure to Sydney or Melbourne branch.

Recognising and tackling the drivers' problem was another triumph for Ken Thomas. However, this time he was the second operator to do so. Colliers had beaten him to it with a depot a bit further south.

Two of the new Leylands, loaded and ready to go.

TRANSPORT CHAOS

1951 was Jubilee year. It was 50 years since Federation; the formation of the Commonwealth of Australia.

It was a year of celebration as people looked back on what had been achieved, despite and including the challenges and hardships of two world wars and a depression. It was a year of stocktaking and looking ahead.

Truck & Bus Transportation an excellent magazine printed monthly since 1937, ran a special feature story on the Jubilee outlook.

They said in the February issue: *"1951. Australia's Jubilee Year—will be seen as a crucial year in the Nation's development, if measured by the yardstick of transportation, the lifeblood of a Nation. With a steady deterioration of international conditions on the one hand, and an ambitious attempt to boost the development of the country on the other, the whole pattern is a challenge to the Governments of the Nation to quickly overcome their short pants psychology of the present day and approach matters with a more mature reasoning than hitherto."*

The railways were caught in a whirlpool of finance and shortages. They could not cope with the freight that had to be moved, yet doggedly wanted to maintain their monopoly on the work, and kept up the fight with road transport. Service to the public was an unknown concept. It normally took up to a fortnight to take goods from one state to another. There were all sorts of reasons and problems.

The Chief Traffic Manager of the New South Wales Railways had reported on the reasons scheduled trains had been cancelled during the previous two years. The figures were:

Causes	Year to 30/6/1949	Year to 30/6/1950
NO Engines	1287	1746
NO Crews	15	236
NO Firemen	1	1
NO Guards	23	41
NO Brakevans	4	29
Shortage of coal	0	17
Derailments	4	0
Total trains cancelled	1334	2070

These figures did not include the 164 trains in 1949/50 that were not even scheduled to run because it was obvious that there would be no steam engine available.

1950 had seen a 55% increase over the previous year in cancellations of trains that were scheduled but then not able to run.

Darling Harbour rail yard about 1950 with Sydney City in the background.

It got worse. The *Sydney Morning Herald* reported that to move the freight offering, the railways needed to load 27,000 wagons a week, but all they could manage was 22,000. In 1951 the number of cancelled trains rose to 4525.

The *Herald* story complimented the railways on the job they had done with the movement of grain, but said they had not kept up with the need for move ment of fertiliser and livestock.

There were industrial problems with enginemen and fireman declining to work more than a stipulated number of hours per fortnight. The 1949 coal strike had been a disaster for the railways as they were completely dependent on coal for all their locomotives.

There were many failures that could be attributed to the lack of maintenance and replacements, during the war years, of both rolling stock and track. The maintenance shortage had been made worse by the heavy demands on rail transport for the movement of troops and war time supplies.

It was not only the railways that had problems. Interstate shipping was in trouble too. Some ships had been lost in the war and not replaced. Ports had not been expanded to cater for the growing demand and as always there were industrial problems with strikes and disputes. Interstate sea cargo moved fell from an average of 746,000 tons per month in 1938-39 to 617,000 tons in 1949-50. The railways were expected to pick up most of the task of moving the freight now not going by sea.

Ports and rail yards were chaotic with congestion. Trucks frequently had to wait days to unload the cargo they were taking to the ship or train. There were times when VicRail would close the rail yards in Melbourne for two or three days in a week, to stop more freight coming in until they dealt with what they had.

Meanwhile manufacturers were increasing the volume and range of goods they were putting on the market. There was a large pent-up demand for things people had been deprived of during the war. Items that were previously imported were now being made in Australia.

Transport is a great indicator of economic activity. When sales are up, there is more demand for transport to keep up the stock in the shops.

The position in the early 1950s was very different from the earlier pattern of trade. Australia had been settled with colonies, which became cities, scattered around the coast of the continent. In the 19th century the majority of manufactured goods came by sea from overseas to one of these cities. The ships departed with cargoes of wool, grain, fruit, meat and other primary products. Each separate colony had customs gates at the borders, and charged duty on some products. This meant that there was not a lot of trade between the states. Although the interstate customs duties disappeared after Federation, the trade pattern remained much the same.

The Bulletin, a respected Australian magazine, said of the early 1950s conditions:

"The growing confusion, the charges and counter charges, the shocking anomalies, the injustices and selfish arguments between State Governments, their railways, and private road hauliers...Boiled down, the position is that the State Railways cannot handle the goods requiring transport between the four eastern mainland states, neither can coastal shipping. The public owned railways show steadily mounting losses, and the Governments impose taxes to compensate their railway losses...and yet, if there was no road transport the railways could not handle a fiftieth of the nation's goods."

In this chaos Ken Thomas had a small but growing business, and naturally, he looked for opportunities to get as much work as he could.

There were two major problems. The first was the road tax, the second was the variation in the railway gauges in Australia. If only these obstacles could be removed.

The K.W.Thomas Transport Pty Ltd fleet at that time consisted of 18 trucks. Ten of them were on interstate work; four Leyland Beavers, an AEC Matador,

The International KB7 with a single-axle trailer worked hard although it could legally carry only 12 tons. This is believed to be the truck that Arthur Bray was working under at 3am one morning when Ken offered him a job.

and two Federals all with 34' Bogie trailers, a KB7 International with single-axle semi, and two table-tops, an International and a Bedford. There were six trucks and two mobile cranes for local work. At that stage there were 32 employees. Sub-contractors were in addition to these figures. Financial turnover was doubling each year.

Ken and his fellow directors decided their future strategy should be:

1. Concentrate on interstate work, with less local carrying.
2. Develop a haulage, storage and distribution service.
3. Establish more branches.
4. Introduce more wayside hostels for the drivers.

One of the problems in running an interstate transport business is the difficulty in managing the drivers; knowing where they were and what they were doing. Communications in the 1950s was restricted to trunk phone calls and telegrams; both were cumbersome compared with 21st century communications.

Ken's policy was to trust the drivers. The drivers were not given a long list of rules. In fact, there was only one rule: no alcohol while on a trip, and none during the four hours before driving. The drivers drove the same truck every day, and they were encouraged to treat it carefully and regard it as a personal possession.

Financially the driver was to think of himself as a manager, and of the truck as his own business. All the costs were debited to that truck, and the revenue it earned was credited. The trip bonus was a percentage of the truck's profit. Ken said they paid the highest wages on the Hume Highway, and the bonus was on top of the wage. His objective was to have a contented staff. The normal schedule was backwards and forwards on interstate work for three weeks. In the fourth week the truck was in the workshop for a thorough check over, and the driver would have some free time.

At that time all the trucks were open trailers and table tops; pantechnicons were well into the future. That meant that after loading, the driver had to clamber up on top of the load to spread then tie down the tarpaulin. This was difficult, slow and sometimes damaged the cargo. Ken had watched his drivers go through this many times.

Laurie Gurling was a Western Australia driver who had a part load to deliver to K.W. Thomas in Sydney one wet evening. Laurie climbed up on top, folded back the tarp and started to unload with very little light, and without letting the cargo get wet. As he was struggling, another man appeared and offered to help; he stayed sometime until the freight was unloaded, the tarpaulin replaced and tied down over the rest of the load. As they finished the stranger told Laurie, "the girl in the office will look after your paperwork," and disappeared into the night.

Laurie, now sopping wet, went into the office to hand over the papers, and said to her, *"I really appreciate the help that chap gave me in the rain; that does not happen in other places. Would you please tell your boss about him?"*

The girl smiled as she said to Laurie, *"That man was my boss; he is Mr Thomas."*

Ken realised something had to be done to ease the problem with covering loads, so asked his workshop team to construct a metal framework for a truck's tray. The frame was made of welded tube, with wire mesh on the sides and front. The tarpaulin makers were asked to manufacture a tarpaulin to fit over the frame, and then be tied down. This simple idea was new to the industry, so it was featured in *Truck & Bus Transportation*, in November 1952.

Road safety was a paramount concern. The trucks were averaging 36,000 miles per month and there had not been a serious accident. The driver was expected to do the run between Melbourne and Sydney in 48 hours.

Ken found his policy of looking after the drivers worked well. The drivers loved the job, and very few left him. When they wanted to leave it was generally so they could buy their own truck, so Ken would take them on as a sub-contractor.

For the railways, help was coming. The turn around was the introduction of diesel locomotives. In November 1951 the first two Alco diesels went into service with the New South Wales Railways. Their initial use was to haul pas-

Top: The steel pipe frame with a cover to protect cargo.

Bottom: The overhead gantry was used to lift trailers off the prime mover.

Top: An LLV, the NSW rail vehicle specified in the bulk loading contract. It could carry 40 tons.

senger trains, as the railways were still taking delivery of Garrett and Baldwin steam locomotives, which were designed for heavy freight trains.

Although Ken had a leading position in the road transport industry he did not see the railways as the enemy. His boyhood in a railway family, living in a railway town, meant he had a knowledge of, and respect for the railways that now came to the fore. Ken wanted to use rail more, if only he could convince the railway management to give service to win and keep their customers.

To present an industry-wide approach, the companies involved in Freight Forwarding had formed the Freight Forwarders Association (FFA). As usual Ken was the driving force and leader of the group.

With the advent of diesel locos, the scene changed. The railways were asked to adopt a system where a contract would be given to a private transport company to send freight by rail, hauled with a diesel. Talks led to an acceptable arrangement.

The New South Wales Railway would supply a LLV (large louvre van), or MLV (medium louvre van). They were both bogie vehicles, completely enclosed and lockable with large side doors. The companies would have loading platform space at the Alexandria goods yard in Sydney and also in Melbourne, and would pick up, then load the cargo and lock the van. At the destination, the company would unload and deliver. The big breakthrough was that the railways did not charge the commodity rates they had previously insisted on; the rates paid by the transport company would be per ton of cargo. That rate between Sydney and Melbourne was to be £7 per ton, with a minimum of 20 tons in the wagon. There was an annual minimum of 1,000 tons. The forwarding companies were left to set the price for the door-to-door service and the competition would keep them all on their toes.

On behalf of his company, Ken was the first to sign the contract with the railways. Three or four other companies followed.

On 20th October 1952, the new Bulk Loading scheme, as it was known, started. The railways supplied an Alco diesel, able to haul a 700-ton train. There were no four wheel trucks on the train so it was able to reach 60mph. The LLVs and MLVs had eight wheels on two bogies which could take curves faster. Because it did not need to stop for water and coal, the train broke the record for running time; it stopped only for crew changes at Goulburn and Junee before reaching Albury. The train had an established timetable and was scheduled to be in Albury early the following day. There all cargo had to be transhipped into Victorian wagons with a 5'3" gauge. The railways supplied the labour but the Victorian wagons were a different size so a load from a NSW wagon was broken up. Light cargo that had been top loaded in Sydney was frequently bottom loaded in Albury, with heavy items on top. Ken appointed a supervisor to work at Albury and oversee the transhipment, unlocking and relocking the trucks and watching for pilfering. The way the freight was handled and stowed was an important responsibility.

At first the freight K.W.Thomas Transport had was only enough to despatch a wagon on two or three days a week. However, by early in 1953 there was enough freight to make it daily.

In Brisbane a similar system was arranged when the Queensland Railways became involved. Bulk loading then became possible between Melbourne and Adelaide. Freight from Sydney to Perth went via Melbourne and Adelaide, and that meant a lot of handling.

To streamline the service to Western Australia, Ken sent Adelaide Manager Bill Martin in November 1953 to arrange with the Commonwealth Railways to use special freight cars with passenger type bogies so capable of faster speeds on the Trans-Australia line from Port Pirie to Kalgoorlie. Sometimes these cars were attached to the passenger trains. Bill also appointed a K.W.Thomas supervisor at Port Pirie to supervise the transhipment there. Ken called this his 'Railfast' service. His road operations were designated 'Roadfast'.

The important point was that at last the private transport companies and the railway systems were working together. They each saw and respected the capacities of the other party and jointly they provided a service that was badly needed by the commercial community.

Co-ordination had been achieved, not by government regulation and the imposition of taxes, but by cooperation and good sense.

This was a real thrill for Ken, who had been instrumental in the arrangement. However, it was not finished yet; there was a lot more to come. The railways now had diesel locomotives.

The first diesel electric locomotive built in Australia had been tested with a run from Granville to Penrith by the makers, Clyde Engineering, on 24th August 1951. This was the first of 11 ordered by the Commonwealth Railways for use on the Transcontinental line between Port Augusta and Kalgoorlie. The need for steam engines to fill up with water and coal had been a costly problem for years, so diesels made things so much easier. By the end of 1952, New South Wales had taken delivery of 20 Alco diesels. This gave the motive power for bulk loading.

The advantages were that they could haul bigger loads, at faster speeds, with less labour. The maintenance was less so they could work longer hours.

The Minister of Transport, Mr W.F. Sheahan, said soon after their introduction that "Two steam engines with four men, haul 720 tons in six hours and 30 minutes from Broadmeadow to Enfield, and two diesel engines do the same trip, hauling 800 tons in four hours."

Diesel locomotives of course became even more efficient as they developed, and steam started to decline. In 20 years the scene changed completely. In February 1973 the last steam-hauled government-owned scheduled train in Australia ran from Wangi to Awaba in NSW. It was a giant Garrett, pulling a string of empty coal wagons.

For Ken Thomas, this change was to prove a Godsend and his coordination with the railways was to prove a major factor in his success.

ROAD TAX

The continuing problem for road carriers was road tax. Back in the 1930s the state governments in Australia became concerned as trucks and buses developed to become competitors to their railway networks. The railways had served Australia well and there had been a great advance in transport since the middle of the 19th century. The state governments had invested millions of pounds in capital works and in buying rolling stock to provide rail services to most of the settled parts of Australia. Now there was a competitor on the scene, the problem had to be dealt with.

Each government reacted separately, but all followed the same principle. Road transport had to be confined to local areas, feeding freight and passengers onto trains.

In 1932 the New South Wales Parliament passed the Ministry of Transport Act to give control of all the state's rail and road transport to a Transport Board. In order to prevent trucks carrying freight that could go by rail a road tax was imposed: threepence per ton per mile. That was a large sum in the 1930s; it would double the cost of many transport tasks. The tax applied when the transport was 50 miles or more in competition with the railway. There was provision for the tax to be waived when the railways did not want or could not handle the freight. There were also some cargoes that were not allowed to go by road even with the tax.

The procedure was that a truck owner or driver had to apply for a permit for every load, pay the tax and carry the permit on the truck. Police or inspectors were likely to stop the truck and inspect the permit. What hurt was that the proceeds of the tax were to go to the railways to supplement their income. Had the money been spent by the state governments on roads, it might have been a different story.

Choking of the competition and rewarding the rail monopoly was not a popular course, and not good for the economy either. It promoted inefficiency.

The railways had adopted a policy of charging different rates for different types of freight, known as commodity rates. There were politics in this; the rates often reflected the circumstances of the owners of the goods. For example, rates for hay and stock food were cheaper, because they were often moved in drought or flood, and starving stock were waiting. Then because the railways lost money on that traffic they set a higher rate for the freight that could afford to pay. Wool was charged a very high rate.

Another example was seed. The New South Wales Railways charged 19/6 for a ton of seed to be transported 450 miles, but other goods were charged from £1/18/2 to £10/7/8 per ton for the same distance.

That 'social security' type rating was, of course, popular with the farmers who were valued voters and influenced the politicians to keep concessions in place.

All this was upset when trucks came. The truckies and farmers quickly found it better to send wool and other higher charged freight by road, and leave the railways with the stock feed. Governments responded by making it illegal to transport some goods, including wool by road. The railways complained about the truckies picking out the eyes of the traffic, but the railways had created the problem when they introduced the classes.

Not everything could sensibly go by rail. There were good reasons why it was best to use road transport for some loads. The continuing problem was the road tax, and the transport industry started looking for a way to beat it and so sought legal advice. The industry also wanted to capture public interest and support for their cause.

On 23rd July 1952, a group of truckies put a copy of the Australian Constitution, and other items to make a 56-pound load in a wheelbarrow. Barney Morton, a cement truck driver, and his mates set out to push it from Sydney to Melbourne. On the same day the truckies consigned 56 pounds of other items by rail to Melbourne. Barney and his team with the wheelbarrow arrived two days before the consignment by rail. Naturally Barney had plenty of support from other drivers and truck owners. The Long Distance Road Transport Association, of which Ken Thomas was vice-president, had given their strong support. The stunt got generous publicity, much to the embarrassment of the railways' management.

The Constitution was carried in the wheelbarrow because there was a school of opinion that the road tax was unconstitutional.

The Constitution had been written in the 1890s. It was adopted by the people of all Australian colonies by referenda and took effect at Federation on 1st January 1901. Section 92 of the Constitution was the clause that said that trade between the states should be free. The idea was to prevent the states charging customs duties at their borders. Road transport had not been envisaged when the constitution was written, so the question was: Did this section invalidate a tax on interstate road transport?

Two young Englishmen, Michael Hughes (aged 32) and Ron Vale (33), decided to test the question. Both men had had an adventurous war record. Michael had been a pilot in the RAF, and served in Coastal Command in the Battle of Britain. Ron had been a paratrooper in the British Army, and had parachuted into enemy-occupied Europe, and was taken as a prisoner of war in Austria. Ron made four attempts to escape before succeeding. He found himself a pushbike and was in Italy after the Italians had surrendered, but Italy was still occupied by the Germans. Some disillusioned German soldiers befriended him until he managed to meet up with some United States soldiers who got him away.

After demobilisation Michael went back to his pre-war work in the motor trade, and a long haul trucking company in England. When the Atlee Labour Government nationalised the United Kingdom road transport industry, Michael had to make a decision. Michael's sister had already migrated to Australia so he made some enquiries at Australia House in London about transport in Australia, and decided to migrate.

On the ship Michael had the good fortune to meet and make friends with Clive Sisley, a Sydney solicitor. During the five week voyage, Michael learnt a lot about Australia, including the transport problems. Clive had done legal work on behalf of various truck owners in their clashes with governments over road tax. He was knowledgeable about road transport and the problems of the industry. The ship arrived in Sydney on New Year's Day 1950.

Ron Vale had had a pre-war job in the steel industry in England. After the war, his employers decided they needed a man in Sydney and sent Ron to this position. Then the UK Government decided to nationalise the steel industry also, so representation in Australia was no longer needed. Ron was out of a job. Meanwhile he had met Clive Sisley, and it was Clive who introduced the two men and encouraged them to work together.

In September 1950 they went into interstate road transport. They formed a company, Hughes and Vale Pty Ltd, with a capital of £15,000 and bought a Model R Commer with a semi-trailer.

Road tax eased in 1951 as the railways were so overwhelmed. Hughes and Vale saw the opportunity. They bought three more trucks and employed two drivers. They specialised in running from Sydney to Brisbane and southern Queensland, and won profitable back-loading carrying fruit and vegetables from Queensland growers to the Sydney markets.

With the New South Wales Government giving open slather when the railways were in trouble, their four trucks were busy and they were doing well. The trucks were doing a trip in two and a half days, when the rail time was eight days. Then, in June 1952, the full road tax was reapplied, so three of their trucks were laid up and the employed drivers dismissed.

Hughes and Vale decided to fight. They did this because they knew that 70% of the small road transport operators were ex-servicemen, working hard to make a living and supplying a necessary service. They wrote themselves into Australian history by being the plaintiff in a challenge to the road tax, under section 92 of the Constitution.

Michael Hughes saw a similarity to the situation that had applied in the United Kingdom after the First World War. In the early 1920s the privately owned railways found their business was being attacked by the emerging road transport industry, mainly ex-servicemen, in wartime-built trucks. As they were taking railway customers, the government had introduced a licensing and permit system, to restrict the road operators.

On 7th July 1952, the solicitors, Higgins de Greenlaw & Co. (of which Clive Sisley was a partner) issued a writ in the High Court of Australia on behalf of Hughes and Vale Pty Ltd, challenging the validity of the State Transport (Co-ordination) Act 1931-1950.

This legal action caused tremendous interest in the road transport industry. New members joined the Australian Road Transport Association, and the membership of the Long Distance Transport Association trebled. Money to support the fight poured in from the industry. Chambers of commerce and retailers also helped. The whole business community recognised the importance of this case and the change and value its success would bring to transport in Australia.

On 15th October 1952 the case opened before the Full High Court. All seven judges were on the bench. The New South Wales, Victorian, Queensland, South Australian and Commonwealth Governments were all represented. Five Queen's Counsel appeared along with junior barristers. Solicitors were also in the court, a real banquet for the legal profession.

On 16th April 1953, the High Court handed down its judgement. Four judges said that section 92 did not apply, and the taxes could be charged. The other three judges disagreed.

The problem for the majority was an earlier decision of the High Court, which had some bearing on this case. They thought it had been a mistake but the doctrine of precedent required the court to follow that decision. However, at that time a party could appeal from the High Court to the Judicial Committee of the Privy Council, sitting in London. The court indicated this might be an appropriate course to take.

The judgement in favour of the tax was of course a blow to the road transport industry; so as the judges had suggested, Hughes and Vale launched an appeal to the Privy Council.

At that time Australian lawyers still had the right to go to London to have the Privy Council hear a case to make a final decision. This option was stopped in the 1970s.

Garfield Barwick, QC, later to become Chief Justice of the High Court, led the case for Hughes and Vale against the tax in London. The case was again defended by the State of New South Wales, whose legislation imposed the tax. On 17th November 1954 the Privy Council gave their judgement, saying the tax was unconstitutional and could not be charged.

This decision made a huge difference to the road transport industry and was a major boost to the Australian economy. Road rates came down and so interstate road transport became much more competitive.

The railways had a big shake up, too. On 2nd December, only two weeks after the judgement, the Railway Commissioners had a special meeting to decide their response. It was agreed they would have to lower the rail freight rates to meet the stronger competition from road transport.

The companies with a bulk-loading contract were informed that the rate from Sydney to Melbourne was reduced from £11 per ton to £7 per ton. From Sydney to Brisbane the rate went from £14/7/0 down to £9/5/0 per ton, and to Adelaide a drop of three pounds to £12 per ton. The new rates were operative in four days' time. Surely this was a record in railway response times.

Up to then, when K.W.Thomas Transport had a load going more than 50 miles, Ken took the responsibility of paying the tax to get the permit, normally about $150 for every load. Ken gave the permit to the driver as he was required to carry it in the truck.

From the time the legality of the tax was under challenge, Ken, when paying the tax, would endorse the paperwork with the words: "This payment is made under protest." After the case had been won, Ken was able to find his copies of these receipts and ask the state government for a refund of the illegal taxes, the sum of £246,000. Claims were also made by other carriers and over a million pounds was claimed. Naturally the New South Wales Government was reluctant to pay, and it took another court case to force them to do so.

Just to add some more sweeteners, the Income Tax Department of the Commonwealth Government in due course sought a slice of these refunds. In 1965 another High Court case held that there was no income tax payable on the refunds.

Ken split the K.W.Thomas refund with his two fellow directors, Frank Hammond and Ken Smith, so they each received £82,000, a handy sum for them all.

However, the Hughes and Vale decision left untouched the use of the tax to protect the railways for intrastate (within the state) transport. This was still charged, but truckies were looking for ways to go over a state boundary when they could. This was particularly the situation in the border areas. Freight from Sydney to Albury for example would be taxable, but by taking the cargo to Wodonga, just over the border, there was no tax—a big saving. There were several court cases as a result of transport companies trying these strategies.

Another effect was to make trade interstate preferable to keeping the business within the state. Thus woolgrowers in southern New South Wales would send their wool to Victoria to be sold and shipped, and from northern New South Wales into Queensland. It was still illegal to take wool by road from country New South Wales to Sydney or Newcastle.

One of the arguments against the New South Wales Government in the Privy Council case was that the taxes were paid as compensation to the railways, and were not used by the government for their work in building and maintaining the roads. There were indications from the court that a contribution by the road transport operators for their use of the road would be more acceptable. So now the state governments wanted to find a way to collect some money from road carriers for road works.

The result was that a Road Transport Maintenance tax was introduced in the late 1950s by the NSW Government. This was to apply to all trucks over four tons, at the rate of a third of a penny per ton per mile. Trucks running locally, intrastate and interstate all had to pay. New South Wales chose to identify these vehicles with a new registration number. At that time there was a national scheme, and all states used three letters then three numerals. New South Wales registration numbers all started with letters from A to F. Tax paying trucks were allocated F numbers.

However, the weakness of the scheme was that it was the responsibility of the owner or driver to record his runs and calculate his ton/miles. This tax applied through the 1960s but the system needed so many government inspectors and clerks that it cost more to collect the tax than the sum raised.

There was much discontent with this tax and the effect it was having. Trucks were being discouraged for doing the work for which they were the natural carriers: short trips with general cargo. The truckies became fed up with the situation.

An owner-driver, Colin Bird, and five of his mates decided to act. They organised a road block at Razorback Mountain on the Hume Highway, near Picton, south of Sydney. The blockage started on 2nd April 1979, and within a few days hundreds of trucks joined in. The blockade lasted a couple of weeks, and of course attracted an avalanche of publicity, which was needed to get political attention. Truckies in other states did the same. This won the day. The New South Wales Government abandoned the tax.

The tax system had distorted the transport task. Road transport is generally most suitable for shorter hauls, of smaller volumes of cargo, while the railway comes into its own with big volumes for long trips. However, because there was road tax on intrastate trips, the railways in the 1960s to 1980s were taking small volumes of freight to and from rural areas, when a truck would have done the job more efficiently and at less cost to the economy. Railways are best left with the bulk cargoes of grain, coal etc. particularly when there is rail access to the pick-up point and the delivery point.

Dropping the tax removed this distortion and gave the market freedom to have both road and rail transport with each able to concentrate on its strengths.

The Privy Council decision made all the state governments reluctant to bring in any regulation regarding interstate transport as that would mean another court battle. However, they realised that safety regulations were necessary and a permissible restriction, so they were able to fix speed limits, driving hours, and the maximum weights and measurements of vehicles.

Importantly there was no move to introduce licensing as had happened in the United States.

Ken Thomas had compared the Australian scene to the USA, where the Interstate Commerce Commission (ICC) issues a licence to carriers. To gain a licence it is necessary to prove that there is a demand, with a list of the proposed customers. Then the other companies in the area, who would be competitors, are asked for comments. He found the whole process was so complex that a lawyer is needed. Ken thought it was little wonder that there was little real competition and freight rates in the USA were much higher than in Australia.

Ken believed, and said many times, that Australia had developed the most competitive and efficient road transport system in the world.

"I HAVE A GREAT RESPECT FOR KEN THOMAS, IN
SO MANY WAYS HE CONTRIBUTED MUCH TO THE
FABRIC OF THE NATION."

—HON. TIM FISCHER AC.,PAST DEPUTY PRIME MINISTER

THE RAIL GAUGE PROBLEM

To understand the major 20th century transport problem in Australia it is necessary to go back 100 years to the mid-19th century.

Before Federation, Australia's separate colonies all took some instruction and guidance from the public servants in London. They had little communication with each other and were competing with each other for settlers to make their colony bigger.

Governor Macquarie did much to turn Sydney from a prison into a future city. He encouraged the 1813 crossing of the Blue Mountains west of the coastal plain, and immediately built a road which allowed the exploration and settlement of the land beyond the mountains. This happened quickly. Macquarie's successor, Governor Darling, thought settlement was going too far so put a restriction on how far settlers could go to establish farms and homes. This regulation was not easy to police, and therefore not very successful. One of the major problems was transport, to get supplies and equipment out to the farms and get the produce in to the market. The problems of the vast distances were made worse by the absence of navigable rivers in most of the inland areas.

In England the first railway opened for traffic in 1825 between Stockton and Darlington. When news of its opening reached New South Wales, the dreamers could see its possibilities, but their transport need was much different, so they had to wait until circumstances changed. By 1845 wool was the major product, and the growing of crops had expanded and there was then 90,000 acres in New South Wales producing wheat.

In 1847, Earl Grey, Secretary for the War and Colonies in London sent a despatch to New South Wales indicating his support of a railway. In the following year he suggested a gauge of 4'8½." This was accepted by Charles Cowper, the Sydney leader of the railway effort and, later, the first Railway manager. In 1848 a survey was commissioned of a railway route from Sydney to Goulburn.

There was much discussion in Sydney about raising the capital for building a railway and the role of the government. There was a plan to raise money from the business community and the issuing of shares for a company. That plan proved not successful.

Another problem was the labour to do the work. Transportation, the practice of sending convicts from England had ceased in 1839; therefore free settlers would have to be relied on to build the railway line. When gold was discovered in the 1850s, the available labour vanished.

The lack of local experience with a railway was a major problem, and asking for information from England was a slow business involving a wait of six to eight months. In 1849, F.W. Sheilds, the Sydney City Surveyor, was appointed as the first railway engineer. He reported that in England two gauges had been tried, 4'8½" and 7 feet, but in Ireland they had decided to adopt 5'3." Sheilds recommended that this gauge would better suit Australian conditions where there would be long stretches of track and the steep grades would need more powerful engines.

On 22nd May 1850 the New South Wales Railway Directors decided to take Sheild's advice. They wrote to Earl Grey to inform him that New South Wales lines would be built on 5'3" gauge. They said that as there were no lines in the other Australian colonies this would not inconvenience the others, and that timely notice was being given to them.

On 9th July 1852, James Wallace, the new railway engineer, arrived in Sydney. He told the directors that before leaving England he had made a study of the 5'3" gauge track and found it gave no advantages regarding power, as the more powerful locomotives could be used on the 4'8½" track. The extra cost of the wider gauge could not be justified. The directors accepted this advice and changed back to standard gauge. They then found that in the previous week Victoria had passed an Act of Parliament to adopt 5'3." South Australia had decided to follow Victoria.

The New South Wales Railway Directors were informed that "Both South Australia and Victoria were committed to orders placed overseas for rolling stock for 5'3" gauge, and were not prepared to follow NSW again in what seemed capricious and offhand behaviour and so had resolved to stay with the wider gauge."

In August 1853 New South Wales repealed the legislation for the 5'3" gauge and nominated the 4'8½" gauge (now widely known as standard gauge). The first locomotives and rolling stock had been ordered for this gauge in March 1853.

Above: The first train in NSW.

Right: John Whitton.

In September 1854 the first line in Australia was opened from Melbourne to Hobsons Bay (Port Melbourne). The first New South Wales line, from Sydney to Parramatta, was opened a year later in September 1855.

New South Wales was fortunate in the choice of a new engineer-in-chief. John Whitton, a 35-year-old Yorkshireman who arrived in Sydney in December 1856, immediately took on the governor, Sir William Denison. Denison had a plan to extend the rail lines with timber tracks and horse drawn rail carriages. The cost would be much less he said. Whitton had had railway experience in England and was a man with vision. He finally convinced the governor and a parliamentary inquiry that the job had to be done properly and in the long-term interests of the country. Whitton also predicted the chaos that would result when the different gauges of each colony met.

But it was not all plain sailing, as the tremendous cost to cover the big distances with a sparse population was a constant problem. The proposals that the more distant lines be horse drawn, or use timber rails, continued to be argued. As late as 1872, the New South Wales Parliament debated a call to make all lines south of Goulburn, west of Bathurst and north of Murrurundi no wider than 3' gauge. Fortunately the parliament did not agree to that proposal.

Queensland had by this time adopted a 3'6" gauge, on the basis that it was cheaper. The *Sydney Morning Herald* reported that the cost had been £16,000 per mile for standard gauge in New South Wales, while in Queensland the average cost of 3'6" gauge was £11,400 per mile. The Queensland rail was lighter and the curves were tighter.

Western Australia, being so isolated and with long distances, had also decided on the narrow 3'6" as being the best option. As their lines grew, South Australia also adopted this gauge for their more remote areas.

John Whitton went on to make a tremendous contribution to the growth of the New South Wales railway network. After 33 years as engineer-in-chief he retired at age 70 in 1890. During his time 2120 miles of line were constructed. Many problems had had to be overcome: physical, involving rivers and mountains to be crossed, but also the political: facing the critics who wanted construction done cheaper, or the line taken to the places that would win the most votes.

From the vantage point of the late 20th and early 21st centuries the early decisions on the gauges are hard to understand. However, the railway brought such a big improvement in transport from the horse-drawn vehicles that had been used for centuries that it is understandable that the need for a minimum cost per mile, to allow more miles of rail for the money available, was the formula adopted.

The lines grew quickly and by 1883 the New South Wales and Victorian systems met at Albury-Wodonga. The event was celebrated on 14th June that year, when the governors and politicians from each state met, and with pomp and ceremony, offered self congratulations. Nobody complained about the small inconvenience of having to change trains at the border when the railway was such a big improvement upon doing that trip in a horse-drawn coach.

Connection to Queensland followed quickly and in 1884 the New South Wales and Queensland Governments arranged for their systems to meet at Wallangarra. That connection made it possible to travel by train from Brisbane, via Sydney then Melbourne, to Adelaide. Such a trip would mean five changes of trains would be needed, including a ferry across the Hawkesbury River.

All that within 100 years of the First Fleet.

In the 20th century after Federation there was an increasing realisation of the problems and inefficiencies caused by the mixed gauges. After much confusion about what to do about it, the New South Wales Government appointed a Royal Commission in February 1921, to examine the problem.

The report, six months later, was quick but not very helpful. The commissioners recommended that the standard gauge of 4'8½" be adopted if unification was to be attempted. The estimates of cost they calculated to be £57 million for all lines in Australia, except Tasmania. They also calculated that a standardised trunk line from Fremantle or Perth to Brisbane would cost £15 million.

The *Sydney Morning Herald*, reporting this information, captured the general dismay at such costs:

"Unification has been advocated on two grounds, economic and strategic. The break of gauge occasions travellers' inconvenience; the rehandling that it necessitates increases the cost of freight on goods. We may admit that; but neither the tribulations of passengers nor the extra charges on transport for which it is responsible would in themselves justify the expenditure required for even the minimum scheme. The strategic considerations are familiar....but here again our horizons must be bounded by our resources and the probabilities."

Unsurprisingly nothing was then done.

It was to take the Second World War to reopen the subject. The tremendous delays and costs because of different gauges handicapped the war effort and stimulated the interest and vision of Sir Harold Clapp before the war was over.

Harold Winthrop Clapp had been appointed by the Victorian Government as Chairman of the Railway Commissioners in April 1920. He was born in Melbourne in 1875, and had served some years in the United States gaining expe-

In 1942, wartime, hundreds of men were needed to tranship cargo, much of it needed urgently by the armed services. Freight from Victoria, on the right, is loaded onto NSW rail wagons, on the left.

rience in engineering and railway. Electrification of the Melbourne system had just been decided, so Clapp had the responsibility of implementing that. He had senior management jobs with US railway companies before being appointed to the Victorian position. It was noted that his salary of £5000 per year was the highest paid at that time to any Australian civil servant.

Clapp was responsible for many innovations by the Victorian Railways. The first electric train went into service in Melbourne in 1919, just before Clapp was appointed, but he was enthusiastic about electrification and had a vital role in the expansion of the network. In the United States he had seen the use of containers, which had been trialled there and in Europe.

In 1924 with the need to transfer 400 public servants from Melbourne to Canberra, the new Australian capital, came the problem of the transport of their personal furniture, as well as the office records and equipment. Clapp felt that containers were the answer. Six ton capacity containers were built, cranes erected at Melbourne, Albury and Canberra, and the whole operation went smoothly. The New South Wales Railways pulled the rail trucks carrying the containers from Albury to Canberra, but otherwise had no part in the operation. It was not until 1952 that NSWGR had an active part in providing containers.

When the Second World War started, Clapp left the Victorian Railways, and in 1942 was appointed Director General of Land Transport, coordinating state and commonwealth rail and road transport. There were 12 break of gauge points across Australia, where large numbers of men were needed to tranship cargoes. With this experience, Clapp was commissioned by Eddie Ward, Minister for Transport in the Chifley Labor Federal Government, to write a report, with a long-range plan.

In March 1945 the plan was released. The first step was for Vic Rail to change all lines in Victoria to standard gauge. This would be done with one line at a time being closed for a few days while the work was done. Changing the gauge to a smaller size is easier than to a greater size, because the sleepers are not replaced, and station and other buildings and structures are larger.

The next stage was an Australia-wide proposal with a plan for the conversion of 8,470 miles of track to standard gauge; 16,000 miles of new standard gauge railway; 578 new locomotives and 9,750 new rolling stock vehicles. All this was costed at £200 million.

The new lines were to be Bourke to Townsville via Cunamulla, Longreach, Winton, Hughendon and Dajarra, and from this a line to Camooweal, into the Northern Territory and across the Barkly Tablelands to Birdum, and a rebuild of the existing Birdum to Darwin line.

It was a great idea but the cost was not so popular. The state premiers would have to find most of the money. New South Wales being the biggest state was expected by the others to contribute the most. However, the New South Wales Government made it clear that as they had standard gauge, they would not contribute a penny for railway lines in other states.

So that plan was shelved and the matter was forgotten again.

The next stimulus was the 1954 Privy Council decision on section 92 of the Constitution, removing the interstate road tax. This gave a real fright to all the state governments but the decision for a new look at the matter was made in Canberra.

The leading advocate for this had been W.C. Wentworth, MP, the Federal Member for Mackellar. His full name was William Charles Wentworth, but he was better known as 'Bill'. He had entered parliament in 1949, and his vocal opposition to communism had earned him plenty of publicity. Prime Minister Robert Menzies had not offered Bill a ministerial portfolio, so he pursued the subjects he was interested in on parliamentary committees. One of Wentworth's favourites was the rail gauge problem. Bill's electorate of Mackellar covers the northern beaches of Sydney, where there are no rail lines but Bill was a man of vision, not self-interest.

In March 1956, the Federal Government set up a Government Members Rail Standardization Committee. Ten Liberal parliamentarians, led by Bill Wentworth, spent some months collecting information from all the railway systems about the break of gauge problem and what should be done.

The report, known as the 'Wentworth Report', printed on 2nd November 1956, found there were many significant problems and action was necessary.

Defence was a major consideration. The war experience was still very much in everyone's mind. Brigadier L.G. Binns wrote a report on the problems, particularly the chaos that occurred when the war was close to Australia in 1942 and 1943. Binns said there was confusion and congestion; the shortage of rolling stock was made worse by rail vehicles not being able to move to other gauges. 1,600 service personnel as well as many civilians were needed to transfer freight at transhipment points, when they should have been available for other war effort duties.

The Brigadier summed up:

"Perhaps the outstanding lesson is that the opinion expressed by the Defence authorities in 1935, that from a Defence point of view, the breaks of gauge present no difficulty; nor would the necessity to transfer at break of gauge points result in any cumulative delay to the swift and ready passage of considerable bodies of troops, proved to be as about as wrong as any opinion could be. Even if no delays to the passage of troops occurred, and this is by no means true, the troops were not much use without the vast quantities of munitions and supplies they required to fight with. And, as has been shown, very serious delays occurred in the movement of freight of all descriptions.

We got by, but only just. The margin was dangerously small."

The Wentworth Committee came to the view that the 1921 suggestion of a standard gauge from Brisbane to Perth connecting all mainland capital cities was the only way to go. Changing the gauge on all the rural lines on the mainland was just too much. In any case there were already moves for some of these lines to be closed, and to rely in the future on road transport for those routes.

The committee suggested such a move would entail three distinct sections. The first, the biggest and most important, was Sydney to Melbourne. So a standard gauge line from Albury to Melbourne would be needed. The second section was from Broken Hill to Port Pirie, with a connection to Adelaide, and the third section was from Kalgoorlie to Perth.

The committee had done some calculations and found the total cost would be £41.5 million which should be paid by the Federal Government.

The committee noted that there was then about one million tons of cargo moving each year between Sydney and Melbourne by rail, and about 800,000 tons going by road. They predicted that most of this road traffic could be won for rail. To help justify the cost of the standardisation, the committee said that this change would reduce the need for money to upgrade roads, particularly the Hume Highway, because there would be few trucks and the traffic would be mainly cars.

The Wentworth Report was adopted by the Federal Parliament and early in 1957 planning work started.

The standard gauge line from Melbourne to Albury was completed at the end of 1961. The work had taken four years and cost £2 million more than the estimate.

On 2nd January 1962 the first train over this track arrived in Sydney. The train hauled freight wagons loaded with goods despatched by the private sector with bulk-loading contracts.

Ken Thomas had very good reason to be proud and satisfied that day, as he circulated in Sydney with other transport and railway executives and watched with hundreds of others as the loco broke through the banner over the line as it entered the Alexandria goods yard. He would have recalled his work 10 years earlier in negotiating with the sceptical railway men for the bulk loading scheme and the success it had been; but was now to be so much better.

All the spectators were seeing the results of Ken's leadership and hard work in merging the advantages of rail transport with the energy and enterprise of the transport business world.

The Australian Rail Union (ARU) reported bitterly in its publication, 'Railroad':

"An observer might have been excused if he had believed that he was taking part in a victory for private enterprise. Alexandria Goods Yard has been handed over to the glory and profits of private road hauliers. The first goods train was bedecked with their advertisement; the vans loaded with the goods they were handling. Their agents were honoured along with politicians, railway officers and union officials. Goods were being diverted from road to rail, but the goods were still being handled by private contractors........No serious attempt has been made to seize the opportunity to enlarge railway business.........No extra goods are being handled by station assistants and goods porters... The tendency will be for goods to be diverted from railway workers to private enterprise."

At least they had the final observation right. In the next six months the volume of freight by rail between Sydney and Melbourne increased by 125%.

Of course, the ARU could not see that the decline in goods porters was because the men employed by the transport companies to handle the freight were members of other unions. However, many more railway employees had work as train crews, track workers etc. because of the increased traffic.

The first standard gauge train arrives in Melbourne, January 1962.

The first train from Melbourne was hauled into Sydney with a New South Wales locomotive, having been connected in Albury, and the inaugural train into Melbourne was pulled by a Victorian loco. That was the first time a Victorian loco ran on standard gauge. It was to be over 25 years before these two railway systems would trust each other to allow a loco to go interstate.

The train to Melbourne consisted of New South Wales rolling stock, which had been freshly painted in Sydney, then decorated with freight forwarders and clients' signs. There was nothing to indicate that they were New South Wales wagons, so the Melbourne press covering the arrival congratulated Victorian

Railways for the immaculate appearance of the New South Wales vehicles.

The first through passenger train did not depart until 12th April 1962. That night, the new train was the centre of attention at Sydney's Central Station. Governor General Viscount Dunrossil, Prime Minister Menzies, the premiers of New South Wales and Victoria, all with their ladies in evening attire, and about 160 other dignitaries and the media, prepared to leave for Melbourne. They had all dined well at the Trocadero in George Street, and speeches were made as they celebrated this significant occasion. NSW Premier Hefferon and Victoria's Premier Bolte agreed with the Prime Minister that it was historic that the scheme was completed so quickly, when there were three governments involved. At the Trocadero it was announced that the new train was to be called the Southern Aurora.

Somebody not there was Bill Wentworth. The parliament was sitting in Canberra, and he was unable to get a 'pair' to be absent. To draw attention to this indignity, his wife Barbara paraded around Central Station with a big sign: *"Where is Bill Wentworth."*

Ken and Anne Thomas as invited guests were there. Ken distinguished himself by letting loose his quirky sense of humour. About five minutes before the train was due to depart, with the VIPs still talking on the platform, he called in a loud and authoritative voice, "All Aboard." There was an unseemly rush to get on board, and the train was off. When the train reached Goulburn for a crew change, Bill Wentworth was there; he had made a late night car dash from Canberra to catch it.

On 20th April 1963, Prime Minister Menzies announced the Federal Government's decision to proceed with standardising the line from Broken Hill to Port Pirie. Work had already started on the standardised line from Perth to Kalgoorlie.

Top: W.C. (Bill) Wentworth with a couple of policemen before boarding the Southern Aurora at Goulburn.

Bottom: Bogie change in operation allows a rail truck to be changed from one size gauge to another.

There was another problem of how to avoid the necessity of transhipping freight destined for places not linked to standard gauge: the Victorian Railways came up with bogie exchange. This is possible with larger rail trucks, and carriages, that have bogies at each end. The bogie consists of four wheels on a turntable arrangement which allows the truck to follow a curve in the rail track. The bogie is attached to the vehicle by a vertical rod, into the base of the vehicle. To change a bogie it is necessary to lift the rail truck so the bogie can be rolled out, and then for a bogie with another gauge to be rolled in to replace it. There has to be tracks of both gauges, and suitable cranes.

The railway systems built bogie exchange depots at Wodonga and Melbourne. That allowed rail trucks to go to Victorian country areas and Adelaide. Another was set up at Port Pirie for the change to standard gauge across the Nullarbor. This facility meant that freight from Sydney to Perth could remain in the same truck, but have two bogie exchanges.

The bogie change took half an hour, compared to three to four hours of work to transfer the freight.

November 1968 saw the first uninterrupted movement of freight vehicles from Sydney via Broken Hill to Perth.

The job was done.

The Wentworth plan had been completed in 12 years. The successful project was very much due to the vision and efforts of Bill Wentworth. His contribution was officially recognised with the award to him of an AO, Officer of Order of Australia, in 1993.

This man was the great grandson of the William Charles Wentworth who with Blaxland and Lawson found a route over the Blue Mountains in 1813, and later became the first Australian-born member of parliament.

Both Wentworths made a significant contribution the development of Australia.

The programme for the Celebratory Dinner at the Trocadero included some interesting historical information for the guests.

ORIGIN OF
STANDARD GAUGE

The origin of standard gauge—a railway term signi-fying that the distance between the track is 4 feet, 8½ inches—is lost in the mists of antiquity and legend. This gauge was used on the world's first railway line, the Stockton and Darlington colliery line in England, which was opened on the 27th September 1825.

As the English gave steam railways to the world and built most of the early locomotives and rolling stock, it is not surprising that when railway lines began to stretch out across countries, they were built to the specifications of standard gauge. This historic fact, in explaining why such a unified gauge has come to be widely used, does not answer the question as to how it came into being in the first place.

This unusual gauge was known to the Ancient Roman and Greek civilisations, and even to the Egyptians and Assyrians. No doubt the width was decided in ancient times, thousands of years before the Christian era, on the basis of the space required to keep the wheels of a chariot clear of the heels of a pair of horses. The standard 4'8½" gauge was just wide enough for that. In the roadways of Pompeii the tracks cut in stone for the Roman chariot wheels, nearly 2,000 years ago, are interesting sermons in stone for rail enthusiasts. The measurement between the lowest points of the wheel ruts is the same as the standard rail gauge. The chariot wheels of the Romans, the great road builders, etched a pattern of standard gauge tracks deep into the English earth as the aegis of Imperial Rome was extended.

The Romans gave standard gauge to England, and England gave it to the world.

"DO NOT CONCLUDE THAT I WANT TO DISCARD THE CHRISTIAN ETHIC, IT IS A PHILOSOPHY OF HAPPINESS AND LOVE."

—*KEN THOMAS*

THE THOMAS HOME
AND FAMILY

Despite the time he spent on business matters, Ken Thomas was a family man too. He was fortunate to have a loving wife, Anne, who faithfully supported and understood him.

Annie Jean Muriel Mackinnon, called Anne by Ken and her friends, and Jean by her parents and siblings, was born at Cammeray, very near Castlecrag, on 8th August 1912. She was the younger daughter of Archibald and Christina Mackinnon. Her grandfather, Charles Mackinnon, had come from the western isles of Scotland, a sea captain who had prospered in shipping in the 19th century in Australian waters.

Anne had a good education at North Sydney Girls High School, then she gained a science degree and a Diploma of Education at Sydney University. Her first teaching appointment was to Dubbo High School, which proved to be an unhappy experience. Her pupils, unruly teenage boys not much younger than herself, gave her a hard time. So she decided against teaching, returned to Sydney and did a business course to gain secretarial skills.

After marrying in 1939, Ken and Anne moved into their new home at 7 The Bastion, Castlecrag. This was a new unique developing suburb planned by Walter Burley Griffin, the designer of Canberra. Castlecrag is on Sydney's lower north shore only about 8km from the city. It was designed as a compact suburb with a village atmosphere. Many houses have water views of Middle Harbour. The Thomas house was enlarged in the 1950s and would remain their home until 1986.

There were to be five children. Elizabeth was born in December 1940, Rhody in 1944, Megan 1947, Gavin 1950 and Andrew 1952.

Anne became fully engaged in raising the five children and supporting Ken in getting the business going. She was a good local citizen. The community centre, the library and the local school benefitted from her efforts and she was a moving spirit at the tennis club for 30 years.

Ken and Anne made a significant contribution to their community. They were responsible for building some of the local shops at Castlecrag. Ken was on the Board of the Co-op Society which organised the community centre, and turned up to working bees when it was being built. He raised a loud voice when a local school was threatened with closure. When the local shopping centre was altered to shopping plaza, Ken made his objections known, but it happened anyway. On the day of the opening of the new plaza, a kilted piper hired by Ken, paraded around the ceremony playing a lament.

A local lady who had known him for years said, "Ken did not go gently when concerned with injustice, but was gentle in his associations, and renowned for his generosity and kindness."

There was great happiness in their marriage, but some sorrows too. Ken could not have achieved so much without Anne. It is said that behind a successful man is a loving and supportive woman, and that was certainly true in the Thomas family.

In later years, Gavin Thomas would recall those times. "Our house was seemingly a community centre where everyone was welcome. Who will forget the tennis days, and socialising afterwards? We all enjoyed the fund raisers, the play readings, the weddings, the requests for help. Dad provided very generously for many more than just his children."

There were good friendships with the neighbours too. Next door at 9 the Bastion was home for the Mason family, and on the other side of the Masons at number 11 lived fellow director Ken Smith and family. The three families had young children and other common interests. John Mason, in his late 60s and retired, still lives in the same house; he was taken there as a baby, and grew up there. He remembers the model railway Ken Smith had built under his house. The trains, trucks and containers were all there with the TNT colours and logo. John Mason as a boy was impressed that the two Kens seemed to work out their business strategy on the model railway. John still recalls the celebration in November 1954, on the night of the Hughes and Vale decision. John's father was a very keen sailor, and had won a Sydney to Hobart race. He also had a VS sailing boat, and the two Kens enjoyed sailing with him on Middle Harbour. There were Sunday night card games, and trips away together.

Asked to sum up his memory of Ken Thomas, John replied, "He was a cheerful and generous man, not afraid to have a go."

There was no house at 5 The Bastion, as Ken had bought that land to build the Thomas tennis court.

On the other side of the tennis court at 3 The Bastion were Bob and Jennifer Wright. Jennifer remembers all the Thomas family very well. "They were good neighbours and we socialised together. Ken was a great family man. He was devoted to them all, children and grandchildren," she says. Jennifer was impressed at how well the family coped when problems befell them.

In the early years there was friendship with the Campbell family. Ken had met Ian Campbell, who worked at Monsanto Chemicals, a K.W. Thomas customer. They found that Anne had been a school friend of Ian's wife, Phyllis, and had two boys, Colin and Norman. The two families got on well together and socialised accordingly. In Edinburgh Road lived the Sorenson family with whom the Thomas family made several camping trips to the South Coast. When Ken wanted to build the squash courts, he commissioned Chris Sorenson to design them. At a later stage, Rhody Thomas and Peter Sorenson sailed together.

Ken Thomas had a domestic routine, that could have been the origin of the saying *"Early to bed, early to rise, makes a man healthy, wealthy and wise."*

Nine pm was bedtime; if there were visitors he would excuse himself politely and disappear. At 3am he was out of bed. This gave him some quiet time to read, as he was a prodigious reader. He had a special arrangement with the local newsagent to deliver the *Sydney Morning Herald* and the *Financial Review* to him before anyone else. If there was a subject that Ken wanted to write to the paper about, he would do so then. Before 6am, he would be on the way to work. If there was a letter to the paper he would deliver that to the Herald office in Hunter St, or later to Broadway as he went through the city.

Top: Ken Thomas at home working.

Bottom: And relaxing.

Ken never shirked physical labour. He would work around the house and in the garden whenever he could. Saturday afternoons were tennis time and close friends would arrive to play. He liked squash so much that he wanted others to share his enjoyment and had built the courts at Castlecrag.

Ken's Scottish heritage and humble childhood was reflected in the way he taught his children to hate waste and reuse things. 'Use by' dates were not thought of then, so he just kept using things until they fell apart. He taught his children to be thrifty and never spend a penny unless this was absolutely necessary. Another lesson was to do things efficiently. These lessons he took to work for his employees, particularly in the early years.

After the hard work and trials of the first 10 years of the business, Ken wanted an outlet for his passion for the country. The nature of his business meant he had to live in the city, but he wanted a rural place for recreation. With the refund of road tax money, there was some liquidity, so he started looking at the advertisements in the *Sydney Morning Herald*.

One day he found something interesting: a property at Mount Wilson. This is a quiet spot over 1,000 meters high in the Blue Mountains west of Sydney, but a reasonable 100km, a two-hour drive from Castlecrag. In the advertisement the property was described as "*8 acres, large garden, house and cottage, tennis court, and orchard. This Jewel so like England.*"

Being the 1956 September school holidays Ken promised his family that he would take a day off and they would all go for a picnic in the mountains and have a look.

Anne made up a hamper, and then parents and the five children all packed into the car, now a green Holden. No seat belts in those days. None of them

Ken loved the bush in North Queensland.

had been to Mount Wilson before as it is off the Bells Line of Road. They had a look around the village and asked directions to the property.

To Anne's embarrassment, Ken knocked on the door and said, "Is this the house for sale; may we have a look?" Having liked the house, Anne and the children were given an inspection of the garden, while Ken discussed the price with the owner, Gilbert Hughes. Gilbert, an architect, was an uncle of Tom Hughes, QC, a well known barrister and Attorney-General of Australia in the 1960s. Gilbert and Meg had owned the house for only five or six years, but had decided to move to Leura, where Gilbert died about 1959.

Meg Hughes showed her beloved garden to Anne, and the children were thrilled at the idea of being able to holiday there. Anne came inside excited

Top: *The Mt. Wilson holiday house.*

Bottom: *The Thomas family in 1960. From left: Rhody, Gavin, Ken, Megan (at rear), Andrew, Anne and Elizabeth.*

about what she had seen, so Ken said, "Well that is good, because we are going to buy it." The house was a single-story, sandstone building, built about 75 years earlier around a courtyard. There was another house on the property, known as Cherry Cottage. It had been built as a caretaker's cottage, but the Hughes and Thomas families used it for their visitors. That way more people were able to share it.

Ken the businessman wanted to put the land to good use. So he bought an adjoining piece of land to give space for an apple orchard. This was planted but never came into production.

The family changed the property's name to 'Yengo'. It gave them a holiday house, close enough for weekends and school holidays, where they had a chance to experience country life. Invitations went out to the wider family, the Campbells, the Masons, the Smiths and other friends to have some time at Mount Wilson. Geoff Hammond's family, although living in Melbourne, still remember holidaying there.

After a few years the novelty wore off, and the constant need for gardening when on holidays made the family realise it was time to sell. However, over 50 years later the Thomas family and their friends still have memories of much family fun and happiness at Mt Wilson.

The next holiday house was on the northern beaches of Sydney. In March 1968, Ken paid $62,000 for the property 'Winbah', at 41 Ocean Rd, Palm Beach. This was in a prime position very near the beach. Palm Beach was closer to Castlecrag, so the family were able to use it more.

Another real estate venture of Ken Thomas was 'Woodleigh', a property about 10km north of Narromine, west of Dubbo in western NSW. The 2,500-acre farm had a frontage to the Macquarie River, and the recently completed

Burrandong Dam provided the water to increase production. The Wylde
family had owned 'Woodleigh' for 20 years, and Tom Wylde had established
an irrigated citrus orchard of about 25 acres.

In 1962 the orchard had produced 4,473 cases of fruit. After that the Narromine Citrus Packers, a growers' co-operative, was established to improve
the handling and sale of the crop.

Ken Thomas could see a promising future for the property and his love of
the rural scene had tempted him about 1970 to buy it. He spent big money
to improve the property and make it more productive. The irrigation was
extended to grow wheat, sorghum and also navy beans, better known as
baked beans. Ken was keen to experience some more of the country life; a
working property with a manager was a way to mix the country experience
with a business-like investment.

Ken Thomas may not have known much of the history of his choice.

'Woodleigh' had been part of the 200,000-acre 'Narramine Station', a run
taken up by William Charles Wentworth and his partner Captain Thomas
Raine in 1836, only 23 years after Wentworth with Blaxland and Lawson
crossed the Blue Mountains.

By 1901 'Narramine Station' had become the largest wheat farm in New South
Wales, and one of the owners was Frank Mack. In building up the property
he became a social climber who loved to show off his success, so looked for
prominent people to entertain on a lavish scale.

One such was His Royal Highness Franz Ferdinand d'Est, Archduke of
Austria, who came to Australia in 1892 and accepted Mack's invitation to
visit 'Narramine Station'. Mack quickly found out that the Archduke was not

interested in wheat, but was a keen hunter and wanting to shoot everything he saw. Kangaroos, wallabies, ducks, pelicans, ibis, cranes, black swans, bush turkey, eagles, parrots, possums and magpies. The Australian treasures, koalas and platypus were not then protected, so they were also shot, for the 'sport' of the Duke.

The prey were collected and the royal taxidermist and photographer recorded the kill of about 300 head. The Duke even complained that koalas were not very sporting; they did not run or hide, so he called them pathetic and lazy.

This bloodthirsty man was the Archduke whose assassination on 24th June 1914 touched off the horror of the First World War.

'Woodleigh' was subdivided from 'Narramine' about 1910. Ken Thomas was to find there was no bloodshed on the property but the financial side proved a disaster. As every farmer knows, the weather is vital. It rained when the beans needed sun; the mice ate the sorghum. Ken had over capitalised and had to sack Geoff Hughes, the manager. There was season after season of failed crops, and only one year when there was a decent wheat crop. When that happened Hughes despatched every second truckload of wheat to the rail silo, and claimed ownership for himself. That way Ken was robbed of half his crop.

Having sacked Hughes, Ken appointed Denis Galvin as Manager /Share Farmer, with a wage and 10% of the profits. Ken found the hard way that a property like that needed more supervision and expertise than he had given to it. While a lover of the rural atmosphere, Ken had no farming experience or training, and he was very busy at TNT. The company was growing rapidly, and he had plenty on his mind in Sydney. So he decided to sell 'Woodleigh' and asked his son Rhody if he would go to the property to watch over things until it sold. Rhody left the job he had with Sheppard Wine Tankers and moved his wife and two boys into a cottage on the property. Just as he got there, early in 1976,

Ken received an offer at much less than he would have liked, but he accepted. Ken later calculated that he lost $1 million on that venture.

Ken felt he had a moral obligation to Denis Galvin, who had uncovered the wheat stealing and with the property sold was out of a job. Denis suggested that Ken finance a wheat harvesting business, with a number of headers, trucks and a caravan. Denis would manage it, and follow the wheat harvesting season from Queensland through NSW and into Victoria. It all went well for a year or two then became another financial disaster.

The mental health of their youngest son, Andrew, was a major concern for Ken and Anne. For some time Andrew had a seemingly incurable fascination with suicide. In 1969, when Andrew was 17, Ken and Anne took Andrew for a long trip to Europe. They hoped that some relaxed time together would help Andrew, and they returned home thinking that it had done so. However it had not, because on 3rd March 1970, Andrew killed himself with carbon monoxide in a car near the Palm Beach house.

Andrew had been going to the Central Methodist Mission in Pitt Street, Sydney and received some comfort from the carers there. Ken showed his support while Andrew did this, and got to know and admire the work of Rev Alan Walker, the Superintendent of the Mission. After Andrew died, Ken donated land for the establishment of Vision Valley, a retreat at Arcadia, in Andrew's memory.

Ken was very conscious of the effect of death duties, which had to be paid on the assets of a deceased person. Death duties were levied by each state and had been in place for years. They were first abolished in Queensland in the early 1970s, but as that led to a rush of people wanting to live in or own assets in Queensland, the other states had to follow.

When the company, Thomas National Transport Pty Ltd. was incorporated, shares were issued, so Ken put 400,000 shares in the names of each of his children. The plan was more complicated, because Ken set up Trusts for them, each with a holding company as trustee, and Ken and Anne as the directors of each company. Anne was also the company secretary. The dividends paid on the shares flowed through to each child. However, the parents kept control. This structure was of course quite legal, and an illustration of Ken's desire to protect the family finances if he died early.

There was a surprise in the family when the man Ken thought to be his brother-in-law turned out to be a fraud. Ray Miners, the man making a lot of money selling fence palings back in 1946, had married Ken's sister, Alexandria, known as Lexia. After they had produced three daughters, Lexia discovered that her husband was a bigamist; he already had a wife and family, and they lived in the Northern Territory. Lexia naturally kicked him out and was left a single mother with three young daughters to raise. Ken, being a dutiful brother, came to her aid and bought a block of two flats at Northbridge and gave them to Lexia. The family lived in one, and had an income from the other. Ray was convicted of bigamy and he served time in one of Her Majesty's establishments in Darwin.

Ken's mother, Elizabeth, died in 1961, and his train driver father, Gart, in 1966.

In 1986 the house at 7 The Bastion, Castlecrag was sold, and Ken and Anne moved in with their eldest daughter, Elizabeth. Anne died of breast cancer in June 1991.

VISION VALLEY

Back in the 1960s, there was a very active man, Rev Alan Walker, running the Sydney Methodist Mission. Alan was in close touch with the needs of the poorer people, and he could see the restricted lives they led.

Alan loved the great outdoors, with the quiet and peace of the Australian bush, and realised that many city dwellers had no opportunity to share that experience. He wanted to give them a chance to escape for a while to enjoy that atmosphere.

To provide such a place was his vision; a vision Alan shared with Ken Thomas. Being a country boy, Ken understood what Alan meant, so Ken resolved to help.

A picturesque 73-acre piece of bushland was found; while only 38km from the Sydney CBD, it was in its natural state and had no access road. By buying this land for the Mission, Ken was able to get the project started.

By June 1972, the dream had turned into reality, and Prime Minister William McMahon opened the centre, now named 'Vision Valley.'

Vision Valley.

Since then hundreds of thousands of people have enjoyed their time there. True to its original purpose, those most disadvantaged are welcome, to gain respite from difficult circumstances, to make new friends and gain self-confidence with new skills. These days it is not only the disadvantaged who go there; many thousands of other city youngsters come to know and love the bush at Vision Valley.

"KEN WAS EXTREMELY CREATIVE AND WELL BEFORE HIS TIME. SOME OF HIS INTIATIVES, IN HUMAN RELATIONS AND THE USE OF RAILWAYS, LIVE ON TODAY AND ARE A CONSTANT REMINDER OF HIS EXCELLENCE."

—DAVID MORTIMOR, TNT MANAGING DIRECTOR (1992-1997)

THE BUSINESS MATURES

The property at Balmain was a very good home for a few years but as the business grew it became too small. A 7,000 square foot extension was built in 1951, but even that was soon outgrown. A new place in Sydney had to be found. Ken and his fellow directors decided to relocate to Mascot. Mascot was in the centre of a large industrial area, where many of their customers had factories and warehouses. The rail yards of Alexandria and Cooks River were close by and most of the competitors had moved to that area. It was also close to the airport, but that had little importance to the business at that stage.

Ken selected a site on the corner of Kent Road and Coward Street and architects Dennis Olding and Reed were commissioned to design the building. McDonald Constructions Pty Ltd was selected as the builder, and they completed the job late in 1955. The total price of land and buildings was £51,000.

So in January 1956 K.W.Thomas Pty Ltd moved in to the brick two-story building. The office was upstairs and the ground floor had space for the trucks to load and unload, with access from two covered driveways, run

Top: *The new terminal, Kent Rd and Coward St, Mascot.*

Bottom: *Plenty of space for trucks and cargo.*

through from the front to the back. The docks were 60 feet long. There was a separate workshop for truck repairs and space for storage of freight. While some pallets were used, forklift trucks were still in the future.

As the company then had 25 semi-trailers and many more small trucks, the extra space was a huge benefit.

This was probably Sydney's first transport terminal building, designed and built as such. Other companies were using garages and other older buildings, many of which would not permit the easy access of trucks, particularly semi-trailers.

The company grew so fast that they found this terminal inadequate and more buildings on the site were added. In later years neighbouring properties across the road and up the street were bought and developed as they were needed.

The Mascot/Alexandria area was the hub of the industrial suburbs in the 1950s and 1960s. A competitor road operator, Antill Ranger had their depot on O'Riordan Street, the main thoroughfare from Mascot to the city, and thus on Ken's route home. Quite late one night, the evening shift at Antill Ranger were surprised when an old ute drove into their yard, and a 'scruffy character', in working clothes alighted and said to Lou Williams, the foreman, "I am nearly out of petrol; can you give me enough to get home?"

Lou told the scruffy character that they had petrol in the bowser, but they did not give it away, it would have to be paid for. The reply was, "That is a problem because I have no money with me, but you might know of me, my name is Ken Thomas."

"Yeah, and my name is Reg Ansett," Lou replied.

Next day there were phone calls of apologies, between Ken and the Antill Ranger management, as the companies did get on well together.

The six Leyland trucks operating interstate were based at the Mascot terminal. This was known as the 'Roadfast' service.

The company developed a strong body of sub-contractors, with suitable semi trailers for the long hauls and smaller table-tops and vans for local pick-ups and deliveries. The best of these "subbies" were designated as permanent, their vehicles were painted in red, the company colours, and they got regular work. The casual subbies were used as needed and their vehicles were not painted. This system helped to handle the problem of the variation in the volume of freight to be handled. The company's trucks were always busy. The policy became a 50/50 split, so only half of the trucks needed were company owned. This was a financial relief to the company and there were less vehicles to be maintained.

Each subbie had to pay the expenses for his own truck, so he was self-employed but had a steady flow of work. A new man would start as a casual and would do all he could to gain permanent status. Some of the subbies felt they needed some protection and solidarity as the employees had from a union, so they joined the Transport Workers Union. The union negotiated on their behalf with the company. This agreement set out the rates they were to be paid, based on the number of calls the subbie had made, the distances involved and the weight of the freight handled.

One of the secrets of Ken's success was an absence of industrial relations problems. This was probably a carry-over of his railway family upbringing, and the memories of the horrors of the depression particularly for the working people.

His time at the bank gave him first-hand experience of their trials and miseries, so Ken had an affinity with and a desire to look after his workers.

Back in 1946 Ken had given Frank Legge a bonus over his award wages, and that principle was maintained. Naturally it got more complicated as more employees came along and made differing contributions to the profits. Ken kept on good terms with the unions and never had a strike on his hands. There were some disagreements though. One such was at the Alexandria goods yard in Sydney where the K.W.Thomas men were loading 'Railfast' cargo, and nearby were the employees of other companies doing the same job. They were all in the same union. However, the Thomas crew were being paid a bonus and special allowances and so earning more. The union went to the other companies and forced them to come up to K.W.Thomas levels. When that happened the Thomas men wanted a rise to maintain their margin. So Ken had to find other ways to reward his men.

In 1955, to make the Sydney-Melbourne road traffic easier to manage, Ken decided to use his depot, the service station at Tumblong, for a change of driver routine, to be known as the "shuttle."

Trucks would leave Sydney and Melbourne at 9am and 6.15pm each day, and they would meet at Tumblong. After refuelling, a fresh driver would take over each truck. The relieved driver would have a meal and a sleep until the next changeover, when he would head home. This way the trucks had better utilisation as they made the trip faster. At Sydney and Melbourne Ken had overhead gantry cranes to lift the trailers off the prime mover. Another prime mover would be used for the unloading and reloading. The long-haul drivers went home and others attended to the loading, servicing and washing of the prime mover, until it went off again.

The drivers loved it. They had a work roster and could tell their wives when they would be home and what days they would be working next week. That was a rare accomplishment for an interstate truck driver. At Tumblong they had a good meal and a comfortable bed. Should they get caught there on a Sunday, they went fishing in the river or rabbit shooting. The drivers on the shuttle did no overtime so drew the standard wage of £34 per week, plus a bonus—less than drivers who drove the full trip.

The disadvantage was that this system broke the policy of one truck one driver. That arrangement meant a driver took good care of his truck and was responsible for it. The shuttle had to be supplemented with other trucks as the volume of freight varied from day to day and week to week. The shuttle arrangement was stopped in 1961.

The growth of the business meant that Melbourne also needed a new terminal. Ken bought land in New Footscray Road and planned a suitable building. There were then about 100 trucks in Melbourne so the loading dock was 200 feet long and 60 feet wide. It was opened in February 1959.

One of the keys to a successful transport business is backloading. With a profitable load both ways, money can be made. When there is no backload, or the backload is at a very low rate, money is lost. While the loading between Sydney and Melbourne has always been reasonably balanced, the same did not apply to the traffic between Sydney and Brisbane. There was very little manufacturing in Brisbane, and most of the production stayed in Queensland.

Ken studied this problem and wondered where he could find cargo to help balance the loading. He thought he had the solution when he discovered the sand mining operations on the far North Coast of NSW, on the beaches near Kingscliff. The minerals, Rutile and Zircon, from there were mainly exported

Top: *The TNT Melbourne Terminal.*

Bottom: *The Melbourne yard with overhead gantries.*

Top: *The Hume Highway, near Tarcutta between Sydney and Melbourne, was like this for several weeks in 1955.*

Bottom: *The Snowy Daily gets through this time.*

overseas, and other carriers were carting them by road to be shipped from Brisbane. Ken had reason to believe he could change that, or at least get a share of the transport work. As Sydney was a bigger port, Ken could see the advantages of using those ships for at least some of the exports, so cartage to Sydney was the big objective.

Being a country boy, Ken knew that to be accepted you have to be a local, so the first step was to look like that. That meant he had to have a branch, and trucks close by. Ken decided in 1956 to open a Murwillumbah branch, and he found a young enthusiastic truckie, Graham Hartman, to run things from a service station. Graham had several trucks to manage, mainly running to and from Brisbane. Ken made frequent visits to the area, and tried hard to break into the mineral cartage, but had little success. When Ken accepted that the plan was not going to work, the Murwillumbah branch was closed, and Graham was transferred to Brisbane.

However it was later in 1956, when Ken was visiting Murwillumbah, that Graham and the service station Manager, Don Gregor introduced Ken to a friend, Keith Hollands.

Keith although a Murwillumbah man and a fighter pilot in the second war, had a keen interest in north Queensland because his uncle had been tin mining on Cape York. Keith had been up there several times in the previous six years. Ken and Keith found they had much to talk about, and Ken expressed interest in providing any transport services needed if Keith saw any opportunities up there.

1955 was important in road transport history, because that was the year the Hume Highway fell apart. This highway, being the main artery between Sydney and Melbourne, was now being used by hundreds of trucks with heavy loads. The traffic was much heavier than it was designed to carry. In

Left: J.J Maloney (left) and Neil McCusker (right) talk to Ken Thomas (centre).

Right: TNT held a container demonstration for VIPs and customers at Sydney's Cooks River rail yard.

1955 it rained heavily in the Tarcutta area, about mid-way between the capitals. The highway just fell to pieces and became a series of mud holes. For a couple of weeks trucks had great difficulty in getting through. They were held up, or had to take a detour.

During the 1950s and 1960s The Snowy Mountains Hydro Electricity scheme was being built in the area around Cooma, and south to the Victorian border. Ken saw a need for a reliable transport service for the stores and equipment needed by the contractors. He called that the 'Snowy Daily' and every day a truck left the Sydney depot at the same time, irrespective of how much freight there was. That way the contractors could rely on it coming. As the weather got colder this was a more challenging operation. One truck was carrying a tractor blade urgently needed at a tunnel construction, when it was caught in a snow storm. The driver got out, but the truck was delayed for four months until the spring thaw.

But Ken was a railway man. His boyhood gave him an exposure to railway men and he had a great respect for what the railways could do. One of their strengths was to utilise containers to overcome the handling problems.

Containers were just a big box into which cargo could be loaded. The problem always was the necessity to have a crane or fork lift that could lift the container, and such facilities were rare in the 1950s in Australia.

In August 1949 the South Australian Railways introduced LCL (less than car load) containers with a capacity of 5½ tons. They were made of steel and with a tare weight of a ton. They were for cargo particularly between Sydney and Adelaide, and there were cranes for transhipment at Terowie and Broken Hill. These proved to be a big advantage, as the saving of handling the freight by manual labour meant a faster transfer, with less breakage and pillage.

In 1953 the NSW and Victorian railways ordered 200 of these containers for the Sydney-Melbourne traffic, with a suitable crane at Albury for the transhipment.

In the 1950s there was a wider move in the industry towards containerisation. One thing that had to be established was some uniformity in size. The containers had to be carried by road, rail and sea, and not be too heavy to lift.

Ken Thomas again led the way with a TNT container demonstration in March 1959 at Sydney's Cooks River rail yard. The New South Wales Minister for Labour and Industry, Mr J.J. Maloney and the Railways Commissioner, Mr. Neal McCusker were the special guests, with other business people; customers and potential customers were also there.

Piggyback, Port Augusta to Kalgoorlie, in 1958 to avoid the rough road across the Nullarbor.

On display were three different types of container. There was a standard general purpose steel box, 14'6" long, 7'11½" wide and 8'4½" high. The second was a refrigerated container of the same size. Then they saw an open gondola container with drop sides. This latter had been loaded with window glass, by overhead crane at the glassworks, something not possible with a box type container. The insulated container had been tested, and TNT found that the temperature inside increased by only 4 degrees Farenheit, on a trip from Sydney to Melbourne in a heat wave. Just imagine the alternative: a container load of melted chocolate!

In his speech, Commissioner McCusker publically recognised and praised the innovation and work that had been done by Ken Thomas, and all at TNT in moving freight around Australia, and the co-operation and effort they had put into the task. This had resulted in much faster services.

"TNT have pioneered some types of transport services, including the Bulk Loading system, and now they lead the way with innovative containers"

Ken also favoured the railway for traffic to Western Australia. The line had been built in five years from 1912 to 1917 as a Federal Government project, promised at the time of Federation. It had been an inducement to Western Australian people to vote in favour of joining the Federation. The road across the Nullarbor was not sealed and in a very poor state. It was so bad Ken directed his staff and contractors that no trucks were to drive to Western Australia. In 1958 Ken organised a trial 'piggyback' run. A truck with a fully loaded semi -trailer drove onto a railway flat-bed wagon at Port Augusta, and was carried to Kalgoorlie. From there it went by road to Perth. The trial could be done on this track as there were no overhead obstructions, bridges, wires or tunnels. This became a regular practice and many trucks crossed the Nullarbor this way. The railways attached a carriage to the train for the drivers to ride in.

The next step was to reduce the height so that this system could be used in the Eastern states where there were many overhead obstructions.

Ken arranged a demonstration of a semi-trailer which could be lifted off its bogie wheels. On 3rd June 1958, a 14-ton load of paper was loaded in Melbourne onto a rail flat-bed wagon. On arrival in Adelaide the next day a crane lifted the trailer, and another prime mover was used to deliver the load. The modifications to the trailer had been done by Freighter Industries,

Melbourne, supervised by Geoff Hammond, then the Southern Director of K.W.Thomas. The rail truck was a 70' long South Australia Railways car, with adaptions to hold and secure the trailer. This rail vehicle was the longest then in Australia, and could have carried two road semi-trailers.

This system needed cranes at both rail yards, but it aroused considerable interest in the railway community. The NSW Railway Commissioner, Mr Neal McCusker said he was impressed, "I would be interested in propositions from road transport interests on piggyback operations."

However, members of the union movement were not so keen. New South Wales Secretary of the Australian Railways Union, Dr Lloyd Ross, said that the union would declare black any piggyback system that was placed at the disposal of the private road hauliers. He said that the road operations, moving freight to and from the terminals, should be done by railway-owned motor trucks.

In 1958 Ken decided that it was necessary to change the name of the company, as it was past the time for his name only. He wanted the new name to not include Thomas, but the other directors pointed out that it was necessary to have some continuity and identify to the public that it was the company they knew as K.W.Thomas.

It was Operations Manager and Director Ken Smith who had the idea that it be Thomas National Transport, but in short: TNT.

This of course was a brainwave as TNT was in the public mind an explosive, plenty of fire, smoke and action. It caught attention. Not a bad image for a transport company.

As from 1st July, 1958
AUSTRALIA'S BIGGEST INTERSTATE TRANSPORT ORGANISATION
changes its name!

The Interstate Rail and Road Transport business formerly trading as

K. W. THOMAS
(SYDNEY) PTY. LTD.

will be changed to . . .

T·N·T·

THOMAS NATIONAL TRANSPORT
(SYDNEY) PTY. LTD.

Same business, same management, same service — under a simpler and more descriptive name.

RAILFAST ➤

Our "Freight-er" door-to-door rail system, now known as "Railfast", operates from our special railhead sidings in all Capital Cities. "Railfast" vans, loaded and locked by special Staff. **Daily** departures of fast diesel trains throughout our Australia-wide Branch organisation. Transhipment — at Albury, Port Pirie or Kalgoorlie — supervised by own, full-time, salaried staff. Very low rates available to consistently big senders. Phones MX4521, MX4434.

ROADFAST ➤

Our Interstate Road Transport service will in future be known as "Roadfast". Our modern diesel semi-trailers depart daily to all Capitals. Reliable door-to-door service at competitive rates. No terminal re-handling costs. Shuttle service between Sydney and Melbourne. Drivers change at our South Gundagai (Tumblong) Halfway House. We are carriers — not agents; we own the trucks that do the work. Phones MU4521, MU4254, MU4164.

The advertisment for the name change, 30th June 1958.

121

On 30th June 1958 newspapers carried an advertisment:

"As from 1st July 1958, Australia's Biggest Interstate Transport Organisation changes its name!"

The name change was accompanied by a colour change for the trucks and signs. Having hundreds of trucks on the streets was a great advertising opportunity, so an eye catching, distinctive but attractive logo and colour scheme was needed.

Ken had done some business with a Sydney printing company, W.J. Cryer Pty Ltd. So he consulted them. Mrs Mary Cryer was a graphic artist, and it was she who designed a new logo and colour scheme for the company. The dark red of the past was replaced with orange and white, and the logo was to be three boxes containing the letters TNT in red.

The company adopted the slogan, *"Every state, Every day."* Those four words said it all.

Recognition and praise for Ken and his team was repeated when the railway commissioners from all states, the commonwealth and New Zealand had their annual conference in 1959. Their summary news release said, *"Bulk loading and container use and development were some of the radical changes that had helped the railways improve their operating techniques."*

In 1961 the Thomas National Transport Pty. Ltd. directors decided that the company should become a public company and so be floated on the stock exchange. This meant that anybody could buy and sell the shares, and that extra capital could be raised from the sale of more shares. Another big advantage was that the shares would have a publicly known value that could alter daily, and that made it easier to make a takeover. When taking over another transport company, there was usually a component, sometimes as much as 100%, when payment was made in Thomas National Transport shares rather than cash. Listed shares were more acceptable than non-listed shares. The value was set on a public market, and the shares could be traded easily.

At this time the Federal Government came into the picture. The public holding company was to be registered in the ACT, and when asked to approve of the name they took exception to a company including the word 'national' in their name.

So going to the top, Ken made an appointment to see the Federal Attorney-General, Sir Garfield Barwick, as he was responsible for this decision.

Sir Garfield had been a well known Queen's Counsel, or senior barrister, who had led the legal team acting for the transport industry in the Hughes and Vale case in London. Winning that case was a triumph for Ken and the rest of the Australian transport industry, so he was held in very high regard. Sir Garfield had later decided to enter politics as a Liberal MP in the seat of Parramatta. Prime Minister Menzies quickly gave Barwick the Attorney-General portfolio.

Ken met Sir Garfield and pointed out that there were a number of other public companies in Australia with 'national' in their name. Sir Garfield agreed that was the case, but said that the government had decided to not allow any more as they felt a company name should not imply that the business was government owned or managed. The TNT directors had decided that they could substitute the word 'nationwide' instead of 'national', and Sir Garfield agreed that would be acceptable.

So Thomas Nationwide Transport Ltd was floated on the Sydney and Melbourne stock exchanges with a par value of five shillings.

It was now over three years since the name and colour change and the vehicles and premises had all been painted and sign-written. There was then a need to change the name on hundreds of trucks and all the depots and premises. That signwriting job took a few years.

Ken regarded the employees as his family and he took a paternal interest in them and gave fatherly advice as he thought appropriate. The public company gave him the chance to really involve his employees. Ken made an offer to help them buy shares.

Every employee was able to buy £100 worth of shares at par. That meant 400 shares. Ken knew most of them would not have a spare £100, so he personally loaned them the money, at no interest. The employees owned the shares, and would receive the dividends and could sell the shares on the stock exchange. The repayments to Ken were made by a deduction from their wages.

This was a very generous scheme, and it brought the employees loyalty to the company. They gave respect and affection for Ken, that is rarely seen in business.

BRIAN BERTWISTLE

When Brian completed his National Service in 1955, he took up the suggestion from a fellow 'Nasho' to get a job with K.W.Thomas, as they had a bright future. Brian started as a truck driver in Brisbane, then became a leading hand, and by 1961 was in charge of 30 men.

When Ken Thomas made the share offer, Brian jumped at it. He married Nicky, and in due course they became the parents of four children. When the twins arrived, Nicky found their washing machine was not up to the job, and their money was very tight. Nicky and Brian decided to sell the TNT shares. The shares had gone up in value, so they could pay back to Ken what was still owing on the purchase, and had enough for a new machine. Over 50 years later they still express their gratitude.

Brian went on to be an executive with a leading role for TNT in Queensland. In 1997 he transferred to Toll when many of the TNT companies were bought by them.

Brian took an important part in the industry as a Director of the Queensland Trucking Association, and particularly concentrated on training young people to give them skills to gain employment in the transport industry. In 2005 he received the ATA (Australian Trucking Association) Award for an outstanding contribution to the Road Transport Industry. In 2008 he was awarded an AM (Order of Australia) for service to the transport and logistics industry, and particularly to the educational programmes, and vehicle safety initiatives.

In 2012 Brian was inducted to the Transport Hall of Fame at Alice Springs. Brian proudly testifies that his success and contribution to the industry was a direct result of the inspiration and encouragement given to him by Ken Thomas.

Ken Thomas had much experience as an innovator and his leadership skills meant he had a great desire to encourage others to come up with new ways of doing things. Ken sent this memo to his managers:

PROVEN TECHNIQUES OF HOW TO KILL AN IDEA SUCCESSFULLY

1. *Ignore it. Dead silence will intimidate all but the most hardened proponents.*

2. *See it coming and dodge, change the subject, or close the meeting.*

3. *Scorn it. Say "you aren't really serious about that, surely" and get in before it is explained.*

4. *Laugh it off. "That's a good one"*

5. *Praise it to death. By the time you have expounded it for five minutes everyone will be bored with it.*

6. *Mention that it has never been tried so cannot be any good.*

7. *Prove that it is not a new idea.*

8. *Observe that it does not fit company policy.*

9. *Talk about how much it will cost.*

10. *Use the "Oh we have tried that before" gambit. Particularly good if the proponent is a newcomer.*

11. *Cast the right aspersion. Make it look silly or flippant.*

12. *Find a competitive idea to block it. But that can be dangerous.*

13. *Produce 20 reasons why it will not work. Outnumber the reasons advanced about how it will work.*

14. *Modify it out of existence. Suggest changes and conditions so that it will not work.*

Two Western Australian subbies proudly show off their trucks.

Ken sent another memo because he felt the growth of the company had meant there was a loss of the human touch and personality that was there in earlier days. He had noticed in some branches that the relationships between the manager and his staff were not friendly. Ken thought they should all be on Christian name basis, and not the formal Mister.

His conclusion was, *"I think that our successful managers are those who genuinely and sincerely get onto common ground with all of their fellow employees in a cheerful, friendly atmosphere of mutual recognition. The stand-offish manager has no place in TNT."*

"TNT HAVE PIONEERED SOME TYPES OF TRANSPORT SERVICES, INCLUDING THE BULK LOADING SYSTEM, AND NOW THEY LEAD THE WAY WITH INNOVATIVE CONTAINERS."

—*NEAL MCCUSKER, NSW RAILWAYS COMMISSIONER*

TRANSPORT IN FULL BLOOM

The listing of TNT on the stock exchange, together with the change of name and colours, led to some real growth. The company had a new, fresh image and was becoming widely respected in the business community all over Australia.

Evidence of this comes from the figures for the year to 30th November 1964.

The total number of interstate consignments by member companies of the National Freight Forwarders Association was 5,125,000. Of these TNT carried 32.13%. There were seven competitor companies in the N.F.F.A so the other two-thirds was shared by them. Very clearly TNT was the leader, way out in front of the pack.

Ken's policy to establish their own branches was really proving successful. Each branch was to pay its own way and make a profit; Ken Thomas and the senior managers maintained control. At the same time the necessity to provide customer service was never forgotten.

The branches in Melbourne, Adelaide and Brisbane led the way. While Sydney was the head office, a Sydney manager was appointed to run the local operations. So Sydney was also a branch. In 1965, 20 branches were operating. They were in Newcastle, Wollongong, Canberra, Wagga and Bathurst in NSW, and in Queensland: Cairns, Townsville, Mackay, Rockhampton, Gladstone and the Gold Coast. Victoria had Shepparton and Geelong, and Tasmania branches in Hobart, Launceston and Devonport. Adelaide was the only South Australian branch and Perth was on its own in the west.

When the Newcastle branch opened at a service station in 1959, Jack McWilliams noticed TNT's arrival in the second-largest NSW city. Jack and his brother had been running their own truck on interstate haulage but found it hard work with a low return. When TNT appeared Jack saw the opportunity, bought a smaller truck and arranged to be a subcontractor. Being ambitious, he also helped with the daily routine of sorting and loading freight. By 1961 Jack had been appointed manager of the Newcastle branch of TNT, and retained that job for 35 years until he retired. Jack at age 81 says he had a very satisfying working life. There was good money, and a wonderful time, working for Ken Thomas, a man he got to know very well and greatly respected.

Jack recalls with pride winning the electric light globe distribution contract. Newcastle was home to ELMA, (Electric Light Manufacturers Association), and this factory made all the globes for all the companies, Australia wide. For many years Brambles had the job of taking the globes to the rail yard, which in 1960 they still did with horse-drawn wagons. Transport by rail to other cities was slow, and damage was high, so TNT was able to win the work, which Jack remembers was very profitable. The trick was to have a heavy base load with the fragile globes on top.

The relationship with ELMA grew to there being cricket matches, TNT vs ELMA. Jack told Ken Thomas about this and Ken drove the 150km from Sydney to strengthen the TNT team and enjoy the day. The Newcastle branch grew to a staff of 40 people. This was quite an achievement in this industrial city that was also the birthplace of Toll, Brambles, and other well-known local companies many years earlier.

In each case the branch was opened as the need and the opportunity arose. Thus Shepparton was to handle the tinned fruit from that area when TNT won that contract. Bathurst was to service the Edgell's factories. Sometimes the branch was created when a local company was bought.

In 1964 negotiations led to PE Power of Wagga becoming a part of the TNT family and a branch, bringing the work and goodwill Powers had accumulated.

The Wood Transport Group of the Gold Coast was acquired on 1st July 1964, and continued under that name as a TNT branch.

Ken wanted the world to know that he had an objective of 40 branches. He had a map drawn and printed in 1965 to show the present and future locations. The maps were in two sizes and he sent them to the branches for them to distribute to clients, but also for the walls of offices, high schools, universities, and wherever possible.

By June 1967 there were 32 branches, and with another 18 proposed the target had grown to 50 branches. Using the 1966 census population figures another colourful map was produced and distributed.

This map proclaimed Five Facts:

FACT 1. 86% of Australians live in 4% of the total land mass.

FACT 2. 80% of Australians live within 80 miles of the coast.

FACT 3. 50% of Australians live within 80 miles of Sydney and Melbourne.

FACT 4. TNT's 32 branches at present serve 77% of the population. Using $15 million worth of buildings and equipment, our staff of 3,000 provide an Australia-wide network of transport and warehousing services that are unsurpassed anywhere in the world for speed, efficiency and price.

FACT 5. In this highly competitive industry, interstate freight rates are now lower than at any time since 1946. No other major industry in Australia has achieved such a record.

Ken was justifiably proud of his branch network. As the policy was that each manager had to run his branch and was responsible for it to make a profit, there had to be a measuring stick. As the branches varied so much in size and the work they did, comparisons just measuring profit in money terms was difficult. Ken decided that the target should be a percentage of the capital used. 10% was set as a minimum acceptable return. This way a manager had to think long and hard before he asked head office for approval to buy more capital equipment. He had to be sure the new asset would cover its operating costs and the minimum profit margin.

There had to be regular reports, some information weekly, other items monthly to Ken, as Managing Director at head office. Each branch was also debited with a figure as their contribution to the head office costs.

Getting accurate and full picture reports was sometimes a problem. In 1965, Ken wrote a memo to his executives headed:

1. The Truth

2. The whole Truth

3. Nothing but the Truth.

The memo said that a report he had received the previous month from Sydney Branch was a glowing document for (1) & (3). The problem was it had failed in (2) and said nothing about the Chullora debacle, which resulted in a loss of £9,000. Ken was not happy about that.

The branch had to make its own sales to win customers and set the best rate possible. However, in most cases every job had to be shared with another branch, as each consignment went to another place, and another branch would have to make the delivery. A continuing problem was the share of the revenue for each branch. This had to be agreed and set to the satisfaction of each branch manager, and as the circumstances and physical needs of the consignments often varied this was not always easy.

The managing director had also to watch that the branches were fair with each other in service, and that they did not give priority to their own customers and leave until later delivery of cargo won by another branch.

As the branch structure grew Ken introduced another management level, by appointing area managers. Ken delegated some authority to these executives over the branches in a geographical area. They were closer to their branches and were able to help the branch managers as needed.

To make it possible for the branch manager to concentrate on winning business and giving service, Ken established a separate company to be the property landlord. All the freehold properties were owned by this company, and all the leases were in that company's name. All the property management matters were handled by them. Thus responsibility for repairs and maintenance, payment of rates and insurance etc. were all taken from the branch manager and left to a separate team. The branch was debited with a monthly rental to cover the property costs. The annual rent was 15% of the capital value of the property.

Another initiative was establishment of a printing company at head office. When a manager needed printing work he had to get two quotes from local printers and send them to head office. Head office would do the job at the lowest price quoted.

Purchase of trucks and equipment was also arranged by the head office mechanical team.

Adequate and attractive wages that are fair to both parties is always important in every business. Ken was not a greedy man, not the type to be mean and unreasonable with wages. However he did want to make money; that is why he started the business. Right from the start he had paid his staff more than was legally required, but that became more difficult as the number of employees grew. In December 1964 he sent a head office circular to his executives outlining his policy and requesting their thoughts on the subject.

Ken said that the policy should be:

(a) The Basic rate on which overtime was based, to be the Award, plus a years of service payment. This would be an extra for each year in employment up to a maximum to be decided.

(b) A profit share, to be paid monthly, to be credited to an MLC Insurance/Retirement policy, or a TNT Savings account or paid in cash.

(c) Elimination of the Super scheme for overtime earning employees. That scheme was not popular with the men and was not proving an incentive. The figure was £3 per month and should be given in another way.

Branch managers had some authority with wages, and awards varied from state to state, but Ken was anxious there be some standards.

Ken also had a policy on donations to various appeals. There are many worthwhile causes targeting businesses when they are trying to raise money. A lady from St Ives, a Sydney suburb, had written to Ken, and he replied:

Dear Mrs xx

It is a little difficult to decline the request which you have made on behalf of the Bush Brothers. TNT has a firm policy on this—we never give anything to anyone except to the shareholders and the staff. It was different when one had a personal business, but now that one is a paid manager with a very small shareholding in a public company then I really think it would be incorrect for the management or even the board to allow charitable donations. I know that this is not a common practice—but I think it is right. Maybe you would agree that the head of a public service department should not be permitted to give away taxpayers' money. I think I am in the same position with shareholders' money.

All terribly austere, but that is business as I see it. Would you mind passing on the enclosed personal donation to the Bush Brothers?

Sincerely, Ken Thomas

A copy of this letter was sent to the manager of every branch, with the instruction that this is the way to deal with requests. However Ken told them they could send a personal cheque if they wished to, and reimburse themselves from petty cash, to a maximum of $10.

Ken developed the branch structure as the way to offer a very wide distribution service. A company distributing their products Australia-wide could be given a very good service with all, or a large proportion in TNT's hands. Those goods might be collected from the client's factory or warehouse already packed for transit. However, an option would be for TNT to take the stock in bulk to a TNT store and distribute from there as the customer's orders came in.

In 1962 TNT bought Scarf's Warehousing Pty Ltd which brought them into the railhead warehousing and distribution field. This gave the company a new task: the holding of stock for the customer until the items were sold and ready to be delivered to the buyer. For this TNT charged a handling fee, a per week storage fee, then a delivery fee. The TNT office would have space for the customers' sales representatives, with telephone, teleprinter and message services. This really locked in major companies as it gave them fast service, without the cost of establishing their own warehouses. TNT looked after the products all the way from factory to retailer.

Ken prepared a schedule of when the branches would be operative. This showed that by June 1966 there would be a TNT delivery service to and within the city or town where 81% of the Australian population would be living. That was an impressive plan for his salesmen to show a company wanting their products sold Australia-wide.

Given the distances involved, such a service was quite a feat. Again it was a long way better than his competitors could offer. To provide a nationwide

The Brisbane fleet in 1969.

service others would all have to use many agents and subcontractors, and they would have different standards of service and want different money for the job.

In January 1964, Ken made two important decisions. The first was to vacate the field of furniture removals which he had toyed with. He had found that was a specialised field and did not fit into his operations. The customers in the main were completely different to his business customers for general freight. Ken arranged with Wridgways that the furniture TNT had taken for storage in both Sydney and Melbourne would be transferred to them and future furniture removal enquiries would be referred to them.

The second would prove to have far reaching consequences. Ken was asked by Peter Abeles to join him in an overnight express road service. Peter was the Managing Director of Alltrans Pty Ltd, a transport company that had grown quickly since its establishment in 1950.

Emil Herbert Peter Abeles was born in Vienna, Austria on the 25th April 1924. His father was a metal merchant with Jewish blood. With the rise of Nazism the family moved to Budapest, Hungary in the 1930s where Peter finished his education. Peter was arrested and taken to a concentration camp in 1944, but managed to survive. The family then moved to Romania, where Peter met and married Claire Dan, an actress. When Romania became a communist country they decided to leave Europe. In 1949 they arrived in Australia as post war refugees. Peter found work selling books and clothes. He met another Hungarian, George Rockey, and they decided to try transport as way of making a living with two second-hand trucks; the business was to be called Alltrans.

They had heard about the possibility of work at Broken Hill, so in 'Sampson' and 'Delilah' their two trucks, set out from Sydney with no idea how far it was to Broken Hill, or what conditions they would find on the way. They had enough food for one meal, and the trip took four days.

The Broken Hill job got them going, and they worked hard to build their business. Peter and his wife were naturalised in 1954, and became Australian citizens.

Now Peter was getting the measure of Australia and he wanted to get into express overnight parcel services. He had watched with interest a company called Kwikasair, started by Walter Shapaloff. Kwikasair offered an express road service with guaranteed overnight service to an adjoining capital city. There were then two interstate airlines, TAA and Ansett, and Federal Government policy did not allow any others. Having a comfortable duopoly arrangement gave the airlines no incentive to give importance to air freight, so their service was bad and their rates high. Consequently the business community was ready for an express road service.

Ken Thomas and Peter Abeles agreed that it was a market that fitted well with their existing clients, and they should give it a try. They formed a different company, called it Comet Overnight Express Pty Ltd., and decided that they should use subcontractors rather than buy more trucks. The service would be between Sydney, Melbourne, Adelaide and Brisbane. TNT would manage Comet in Melbourne and Adelaide, while Allltrans would look after Comet in Sydney and Brisbane.

There was another competitor known as IPEC, originally named Interstate Parcel Express Company. This Adelaide company had interstate and local services, and was bought by Gordon Barton and Greg Farrell in 1962. However, there was room for another company and its well-known parents gave Comet the status needed to win the confidence of hesitant customers.

Comet went on to become a great success, and Ken and Peter got to know each other well.

1964 also saw some changes for transport to and from Tasmania. Being an island has always been a handicap when it comes to transport for this beautiful state. Things improved when the roll on, roll off concept arrived and the

CHAPTER 9

Princess of Tasmania was Australia'a first 'Roll off, Roll on' ship.

Princess of Tasmania went into service in 1959. That was primarily for passengers and their cars, and so it was followed by the *Bass Trader* for freight. Both ships travelled between Melbourne and Devonport, and were operated by the commonwealth government-owned ANL (Australian National Line). There were other traditional type ships also running.

In July 1964, the *Seaway Queen* came onto the scene. She was a cargo-only ship, and was responsible for a big upgrade in the equipment used by the transport industry to Tasmania. There were new quick release semi-trailers. One prime mover loaded the trailers and another prime mover unloaded at the destination. There were new containers, many specially designed for

The Seaway Queen between Melbourne and Hobart.

Tasmanian service. The problem was the in balance of loading. Most of the freight from Tasmania was large items that could not fit or be easily loaded into a metal box, items like large reels of paper and metal ingots. A collapsible container, a tray with removable sides, became the answer as about eight of these when empty could be nested together to save space.

TNT was only one of the companies offering transport to Tasmania; there were 10 others with cargo on the *Seaway Queen's* maiden voyage. It was a competitive business. While they all paid the same sea freight rate to the Union Steam Ship Company, owners of the ship, the prices charged for the door-to-door service varied considerably.

Unloading the Empress of Australia in Tasmania.

In September 1964 the sister ship *Seaway King* arrived and established a service from Sydney: the first roll on, roll off ship on that route.

Sydney was even better served when the *Empress of Australia,* another ANL ship came onto the run with its maiden voyage in January 1965. More Tasmanian ports were served as she rotated between Hobart, once a fortnight, and Bell Bay and Burnie, twice a fortnight.

Tasmania was on the map.

On the mainland competition was running hot. For the year 1st July 1963 to 30th June 1964 there was an increase of 300,000 tons of freight moved by rail between Sydney and Melbourne, making a total of one and a half million tons. However the road figures were not far behind; trucks carried 1,430,528 tons in that year. In the first year of standard gauge, between Sydney and Melbourne there was a 145% increase in rail traffic southbound, and 115% northbound. To the surprise of the industry, the road traffic was very stable and had declined by only 3.8%. Clearly there was a big increase in the total freight task.

Ken Thomas, being a strong believer of the need to maximise the use of rail, was constantly on the lookout for the way to overcome the need to handle cargo. This was rail's disadvantage. Handling costs money, and increases the risk of damage to the merchandise being carried. That was the big advantage of road transport. Containers were one way to minimise handling, particularly when they were loaded at the consignor's premises, and could be unloaded when they reached the consignee. There were some cargoes where that was not possible, so other options were needed. One of those was the transport of a semi-trailer on a railway flat-top wagon, but that could only be done when there were no tunnels, bridges or overhead power lines. In practice across the Nullarbor Plain was then the only route.

The problem could be overcome when the wheels of the truck could be detached from the trailer, and so reduce the height. That meant a specialised road trailer, and a specialised rail wagon, where a transfer could be done with a suitable turntable. This process was known as a Flexivan, and had been tried in the USA.

The decision Ken had made in 1948 to offer Arthur Bray a job, while he worked under a truck broken down on the Hume Highway at 3am one cold morning, had brought into the business a real mechanical wizard.

Clockwise from bottom left: 1. A loaded Flexivan arrives at the railyard. 2. The Flexivan goes onto the turntable on the rail vehicle. 3. The Flexivan is ready to go by rail.

Arthur had become service manager, responsible for the mechanical needs of all the trucks and equipment, as well as developing new devices and methods to handle freight. In 1963 Arthur was the head office technical adviser, and Ken sent him to the USA to learn about the techniques they had there. Flexivans were one of these.

A Flexivan is a giant container that can be transferred from road wheels to rail wheels, without a crane to lift it. The technique is to have a flat bed road vehicle stop at a right angle to a rail flat bed wagon with a turntable. Hydraulically the road vehicle pushes the Flexivan off, across the turntable, so the rail vehicle has the Flexivan at right angles. The turntable is then used to move the Flexivan along the rail truck. Loads of about 20 tons could be handled this way. There was an open tray version for large items, known as a Flexiflat.

This was a touchy operation, and the weight distribution in the Flexivan was critical.

Arthur Bray visited Fruehauf in the USA, and then with Fruehauf in Australia developed the equipment to suit the Australian conditions, particularly the rail vehicles here. TNT had the first Flexivans in Australia. Ansett Freight Express was not far behind, but they beat TNT to a publicity event showing off the new equipment. On the day Ansett had a big media demonstration in Melbourne, Arthur Bray turned up as well. The Ansett team had a very embarrassing experience with their operation going wrong so Arthur stepped up and fixed the problem. So with TV cameras whirring, he saved the day for a competitor company.

Arthur was promoted to TNT Manager for all of Queensland in 1963, and quickly won the respect of the staff there. A further promotion came in October 1971 when Arthur was given responsibility for all of Western Australia and made the Resident Director.

Being a public company, Thomas Nationwide Transport Ltd had to report regularly to the shareholders, the stock exchange, and hence the public. As Australia had adopted decimal currency in February 1966, the profit figures for the period 1961 to 1965 expressed in dollars became:

1962 $263,000, 1963 $365,000, 1964 $502,000, 1965 $625,000.

At an annual meeting on 30th September 1966, Ken gave the chairman's address, and reported on the year' s achievements. He said the profit for the year to 30th June was $678,000, a return of 21.8% return on capital. There had been major work done on terminals, with $470,000 spent on a new road terminal at Mascot, as well as new buildings or branches at Griffith, Albury, Canberra, Gladstone, Newcastle, and Shepparton.

Ken was also able to proudly remind the shareholders of the amount of TNT freight that was moving by rail. There were now Flexivans, Flexiflats, containers and LLV's (large louvre vans) of sufficient numbers that whole trains were being despatched with TNT freight. "This year," Ken said, "our account with the railways of Australia will exceed $8 million. At the same time we have been wage and salary leaders in the industry, there is satisfaction in saying that Australia and thousands of Australians were better off because of our existence."

The shares had risen in value from 58 cents at flotation to $1.30 at 30th June 1966. Shareholders had also the benefit of three one-for-ten par issues, in 1963, 1964, and 1965. A par issue is an opportunity to buy more shares at their par price, but there is a limit. In this case a shareholder could buy one new share for 50 cents, for every 10 shares already held. That means new shares at a saving of 80 cents each.

Ken told the shareholders that he believed that Australia had the world's lowest land transport costs, and he wanted to do more study to substantiate that view.

As big as the company was, and as busy as Ken was, he never lost the personal touch with his staff. Nor did he let a likely recruit escape. TNT's bank was the ANZ at Waterloo, and one day Ken decided that a young lady there might be able to fill a job he had. So Ken asked the bank manager, did he think Ann Worboys could handle the work. The manager said he thought so, and lost his young staff member. Ann went to be secretary to Ken Thomas and Gordon Evans, the company secretary.

Ann recalls that Ken was "a lovely man, nothing sexist, he treated people as they worked." Although TNT was predominantly a male organisation, he appointed a woman, Gwen Lee, as an accountant. After Ann married and had a baby, Ken took flowers to her at the hospital. He was appalled at the prospect of his office without her, so offered to pay Ann's mother to baby sit so Ann could keep working. But it did not happen; the call of a baby to a new mother was stronger than a call from Ken Thomas.

Another who remembers Ken's human side is Gerry Rowe. Gerry was recruited as a trainee manager in Melbourne, and only a few months later was sent to Hobart to relieve the manager there. The big boss, Ken Thomas was coming to town and Gerry had to make the arrangements. There was an evening meeting over dinner at the hotel, time got away and Gerry was entrusted to deliver Ken's breakfast menu to the reception desk as he went down to his car. He forgot. At 3am, he woke up and remembered, so dressed, hopped into his car and drove back to the hotel. Of course it was all locked, so all he could do was put the menu under the door. Gerry presented himself to Ken next morning, and, as feared, Ken had had no breakfast. Was this the end of his time with TNT? No, Ken thought it a great joke and they later enjoyed the day's meetings and the activities that Gerry had arranged. Ken amazed his colleagues that day when he displayed a good knowledge of plants and their botanic names in the Hobart Botanic Gardens.

Phyllis Merrell was a TNT employee for 35 years, and has many happy memories of her time when Ken was the boss. After each five years of service there was an expensive present to the employees. There was the opportunity to buy shares at par when the company floated, funded by a loan from the company, repaid by payroll deductions. Phyllis remembers the ball each year organised by the social club. As the company grew the venues got larger, until they filled the Sydney Town Hall. Phyllis distinguished herself by being the first female sales representative in TNT, and probably in the Sydney transport industry. That was quite an experience in the predominantly male world of business in the 1960s. Phyllis says she felt the need to work harder to prove herself. Husband Colin was also an employee, and told of the time that there was an industrial dispute at Mascot, and the loaders and drivers were on strike. Ken rallied the office staff, and led the men and women to the dock, where they all took off their coats and got the freight moving. "Working for Ken," Colin said, "was like being in a family as we all felt we were a part of it."

Ken was compassionate too. There was a driver, Harry Nyberg, who had been in the family since 1953 as an employee and a subcontractor. Harry died after an accident in Perth, and was well known from Perth to Cairns. Ken described him as "A big, happy, hard-working man. Everybody got along well with Harry and respected him for his essential kindness and good humour."

Harry was a subcontractor at the time of his death, so there was no benefit legally required from TNT. Ken decided that it was appropriate that there be an appeal for Harry's wife. Ken personally contributed $500, the company paid $1000, and Ken Smith, a director who had first employed Harry, gave $500. Ken asked the branch managers to add to the fund.

Early in 1967, Ken was on a high; he had achieved another break through with the railways. After months of negotiations there was an agreement that TNT could lease two BC rail wagons (a flat-top vehicle) for 12 months and the railways would haul them between Sydney and Melbourne as fast as TNT could load them. The annual rent was to be $65,000 per wagon. Ken had been working on this arrangement for months and had offered the railways $55,000 per wagon per year. When time went by with no answer on the new plan, Ken despaired about it ever seeing daylight. As the company needed more capacity to move freight between Sydney and Melbourne, Ken decided they would have to carry it by road so authorised the purchase of 12 new Kenworth trucks for this run. This news obviously leaked because within a couple of weeks, the railways had agreed to the arrangement Ken had been pushing for. Ken wasted no time in accepting and drew up a schedule and timetable. Each wagon could carry a maximum load of 50 tons, and this would be in nine containers on each trip. The rail wagon would do six trips a week, as it could depart from both Sydney and Melbourne at 2pm each day, including Saturday, and arrive at 8am next day. There would be a large fork-lift truck to unload at each rail yard, and load another nine containers for departure that afternoon. Ken calculated that the line haul cost would be only $6 per ton, below the cost of road haulage.

The cherry on top of the cake for Ken was that the other transport companies could not follow them as the railways had only two of these wagons immediately available; he wanted more as quickly as possible and he hoped that it would be a six month start before any wagons would be available for

BC Boxes, designed and built by TNT, come off a train.

his competitors. In this his initiative paid off because his biggest competitor, F.H. Stephens did not get access to these wagons until September—TNT had a five month start.

Marketing was an important consideration as he wanted his salesmen to sell the service, but he did not want his competitors to hear about it. The first step was to build 100 special new containers for this traffic, which would start on 3rd April 1967. The containers were known as BC boxes; they were 8ft x 8ft and were built by TNT.

Ken was smart enough to see that this fast service should be sold at a premium, rather than at a lower rate to undercut the competition. If a better rate could be achieved that would help the company's profit margin. He decided that this should be sold as the Transcon service, with its own general manager and a manager in each capital city. The intention was to get all the BC wagons as the railways acquired them and extend the service to Brisbane and Adelaide as soon as possible.

One of the secrets of Ken's success was his cultivation of his staff. They were regarded as partners and so were rewarded with bonuses, share purchase schemes, and responsibilities. His executives were taken into his confidence and given authority to make decisions. They were treated as family members rather than as employees.

An example of this is the executive conference Ken called together at Manly in January 1967. Twenty-seven of his senior staff gathered from all over Australia for a weekend. They all arrived on Saturday morning, and had a quick inspection of some of the Sydney operations at Mascot and Chullora. The meeting started at 2pm; later there was time for a quick swim before a night out. They were warned to be restrained as Sunday was to be a big, intensive, solid day, which would continue after dinner that night. Some of the interstate men would go home on Monday, others would not get away until Tuesday.

The conference discussed the overall problems of the company, handling large amounts of freight, and how to do this with good customer service and profitably. Ken's report summarised it: *"An unfortunate consequence of our enormous volume appears to be that our huge volume accounts are ruining the quality of service for our high profit, under one ton lots, and we are losing business in this high profit area at the very time when high rate accounts are needed."*

A number of plans were made to help with solutions to this eternal problem for transport operators in a competitive environment.

The conference at Manly.

Standing left to right: Greg Poche, Neil McDonald, Ted Prebble, Harry Burns, John Deegan, Bill Weekes, Wal Ginn, Jim Gardener, Brian Flynn, Roy Heasman, Col Anderson, Chris Johnson, Norm Sturgeon, Dick Buzzard, Graeme John, Maurie Ravet and Malcolm Thomson.
Seated left to right: Len Small, Brian Bertwistle, Ted Johnson, Colin Hywood, Gerry Rowe, Kevin Becker, Murray Gaston, John Hughes, Brian Farnam, Ken Thomas and Ian McLean.

Ken was equally at home with his, 'blue-collar men': the drivers, mechanics, storemen and loaders who did the physical work. A favourite habit of Ken's was to turn up at a depot or yard, about knock-off time. He would produce a large parcel of fish and chips and from the boot of his car came several cartons of cold beer. This gave the men a chance to relax and give feed-back right to the boss. For Ken it was important human relations. It is no wonder that his staff all over Australia thought very highly of their boss, and they were loyal and proud to work for Ken Thomas.

Not many managing directors of a public company could or would do that.

Ken formalised this feedback when he launched a suggestion scheme with a bonus payment for good ideas. He wrote that he wanted to utilise *"the thinking power of the troops."* Original ideas submitted in writing to a suggestion committee could earn a bonus from $10 to $2000, depending on the savings to the company.

"THE GLORY OF ROAD TRANSPORT IN AUSTRALIA IS UNRE-
STRICTED ENTRY. MANY SUCCESSFUL COMPANIES WOULD
NEVER HAVE STARTED IF THEY HAD TO 'PROVE THE NEED'.
THEY HAD NO CREDENTIALS, THEY JUST HAD A GO."

—KEN THOMAS

CARGO DISTRIBUTORS

Ken Thomas watched with interest the merger of several competing companies to become Cargo Distributors in 1962. It resulted in much stronger competition for TNT.

The merger was of several well established companies, Rudders Ltd; Seaton's Transport Pty Ltd; Mercury-MTC Pty Ltd; and Cargo-MTC Pty Ltd and they together became a large interstate forwarding organisation. They also had contracts with GMH for the distribution of Holden cars.

Rudders had been in business since 1896. They were strong in forwarding and customs work, and had done very well with a service to Darwin, using plywood containers. These containers were necessary because of the frequent transhipments of freight, with the gauge changes and the road segment from Alice Springs to Darwin.

The new company was Cargo Distributors Ltd, a public company listed on the stock exchange. There were 20 subsidiaries, companies that had been bought and integrated. It was Mercury who had developed the special car-carrying trailers, now widely used.

To upgrade their Sydney facilities Cargo leased 6.5 acres of railway land at Rozelle about 5 km from the city, then spent £170,000 constructing buildings. This gave them a half-mile railside terminal and offices of 6,800 sq.ft which they occupied in January 1964.

In the other states, Cargo had opened a new terminal in Hobart, and had a 17-acre site in Brisbane they intended to build on. There were also terminals planned in Adelaide, Perth and Launceston.

So having worked hard to put this group together, Cargo attracted the attention of a UK transport company. Transport Development Group Ltd of London made an offer to buy the shares. The five shilling shares had been trading on the stock exchange for 14 and ninepence, and the offer was 20 shillings cash, or a TDG share and some cash. If all the shareholders took cash the total cost to TDG was £5,550,000. The directors of Cargo Distributors decided this was a generous offer so they recommended it to the shareholders. The advice was accepted and the sale was completed.

This transaction had brought Australian transport companies to the notice of UK stock-brokers and investors, and they were impressed with the way the transport industry had grown and developed, and the profits being made. Ken Thomas and TNT very quickly caught their eye. Because of this, the Managing Director of the Transport Development Group Mr W. Fraser and Ken began corresponding with each other early in 1965.

Ken's main reason for writing was because of the rate war that had broken out between TNT and Cargo Distributors. They were cutting prices to steal each other's customers, and the rates were less than cost. Ken had tried to get the problem fixed with the Cargo management in Australia, but to no avail.

Mr Fraser suggested that Transport Development Group (TDG) buy TNT, and Ken replied that the only reason he would do that would be to stop the war. However, the idea had some appeal and for a few months they corresponded on the matter, and made suggestions to each other. By June 1966 they had found an arrangement that appealed to them both; the TNT directors had approved, so an announcement was made to the stock exchange. There was to be an exchange of shares. All the TNT shareholders would be given the same number of TDG shares. The TDG shares were listed on the stock exchange and had been traded at four to five shillings more than the TNT shares.

Ken had agreed to continue as managing director for five years, the operations of TNT and Cargo would be integrated and the cost savings that would result had been identified. All in all it seemed a good deal for everybody.

The catch was that the arrangement would need to meet the requirements of Australian Exchange Control, handled on behalf of the Federal Government by the Reserve Bank. On the 15th July 1966 the bank advised that it was not an acceptable transaction, as it would mean that Australian shareholders would lose their equity in an Australian company for a portfolio investment in an overseas company, which was contrary to the existing government policy.

So they all went back to the drawing board. Some urgent correspondence and cables were exchanged, and on 29th July the TNT directors agreed to another plan. TNT would offer to buy Cargo Distributors Ltd, from TDG, with three million TNT shares and $680,000 cash. TDG would receive $5,180,000.

The Cargo Distributors terminal at Rozelle, Sydney.

A condition was that TNT would remain a public company and a minimum of 25% of the shares would be Australian owned. The TNT shares to be acquired by TDG would be no more than half of each shareholder's portfolio.

There were some adjustments, but the scheme was acceptable to the Reserve Bank and so it proceeded.

For the time being TNT remained an Australian company. There were two seats on the TNT Board of Directors for TDG representatives, and Ken was still the managing director so could now stop the price cutting. But Ken had not gained a pathway to being able to stand aside, something he was starting to look forward to.

1966 was the year that decimal currency was introduced to Australia. That change had been decided by Prime Minister Sir Robert Menzies some years previously and all the arrangements made over several years. As usual Ken was thinking ahead and challenged the measurement system, particularly the aspect that was so important to transport, measuring weights. The imperial system with tons, hundredweights, quarters and pounds was very cumbersome. The calculation of the freight payable on a consignment, when the rate was X pounds per ton was quite a task. There were of course no computers or even calculators to do the sums.

Ken advocated that the transport industry should express weights in pounds and tons. He called this the decimal weights scheme, as used in the United States of America. By simply moving the decimal place the rate per pound was known and applied. Twenty times the 100 pounds would make a short ton. The cubic equivalent for bulky goods was five cubic feet for 100 pounds.

Ken succeeded in getting the Australian Road Transport Federation to agree to this proposal and they took it up with the Federal Government. After he became Prime Minister Harold Holt announced in November 1964 that a meeting would be held of federal and state ministers to consider whether Australia would adopt the metric weights and measures scales.

However, by the time decimal currency was introduced in February 1966 nothing had happened so Ken sent a circular to all his staff saying that from 1st April, all TNT rates should be expressed in per 100 pounds weight.

Again Ken was way out in front. All of Australia did adopt metric measurements, but not until 1st July 1973.

In August 1967, Ken advised the shareholders that the year's profit to 30th June had increased by 41.2%, to $956,243.

The report said that the companies in the Cargo Distributors Group were now trading profitably, although they were struggling at the time of the take-over. This had been achieved by the economies of rationalisation, as he had forecast a year earlier.

POLITICS

Ken Thomas was a pacifist. That was the reason for his initial reluctance to joining the Armed Forces in World War Two.

When Australia became involved with the Vietnam conflict, as a result of the call and pressure from the United States of America, Ken was disturbed. Australia's involvement was a gradual process during the 1960s. In November 1964 the Menzies Government reintroduced national service for young men.

The first National Service Scheme, started in 1951, was for all men as they turned 18; subject to their physical fitness. Those going to the army had three months full time initial training, then two years part time in the Citizens Military Force. That was found to be unwieldy as it yielded more men than could be trained to a useful level, so it was abandoned.

The 1964 revision was for fewer men, but a greater period of service. This time only the numbers that the armed services could handle were called up. They were selected by a birthday ballot; all those whose date of birth was on a marble drawn from a box. Service was for two years full time with a provision that service overseas may be required. The compulsion of this system added to the distaste for the war in Vietnam, a country that Australians knew little about and had little interest in. It meant there was a steady growth of opposition as the war stepped up.

To the United States Government this was another step in their campaign against communism; an issue which was a very strong part of world politics in the 1950s and 1960s. Vietnam was seen as important as the North Vietnamese were communist and wanted to infiltrate other parts of Asia. Australia supported the Americans, so Australians who opposed the war blamed the USA.

As the war escalated Australia, now with Harold Holt as prime minister, committed more and more troops, seemingly as the Americans asked. It appeared to be a bottomless pit, and more Australian people were becoming concerned as to where it would lead.

One of those who worried was Gordon Barton. Gordon was born on 30th August 1929, so was 16 years younger than Ken Thomas. Gordon had a good academic record with degrees in Law, Arts and Economics, and was the founder and Managing Director of IPEC. Gordon had started IPEC, an interstate fast freight service company, while at university, to fund his studies. Although they were competitors, Ken Thomas and Gordon had a friendly relationship. Gordon lived at Castle Cove, not far from Ken's home at Castlecrag.

Gordon was anxious to make his feelings known. He wanted more action than a letter to the prime minister. He had already tried that.

An open letter to the President of the United States of America

Dear Mr President:

It is unfortunate that your welcome in Australia has been clouded by the deep disagreement in this country as to our part in the Vietnamese War. I am concerned that the thought, comment and actions of our Government have reflected very little of this disagreement, nor indeed much awareness of what is involved.

The fact that out of a population of eleven million we have had to depend on conscripts to make up two battalions to send to Vietnam is a sufficient indication that enthusiasm for this war is very largely confined to our politicians and their military advisers.

These are some of the reasons for this lack of enthusiasm:

The Vietnamese War has become known as a "dirty" war. This is so partly because of the hardly disguised cynicism and brutality with which it has been conducted over the 20 years it has been going on, partly because it retains much of its original character of a colonial war, and partly because of the extent of the suffering of the civilian population.

Our problem is to satisfy ourselves that we have some very good reason to take part in this "dirty" war.

Since it is clear enough that the only foreign military forces in Vietnam are those of America and her allies it is very difficult for us to accept the fiction that we are merely helping the Vietnamese people to defend themselves against outside aggression.

Most people accept the commonsense view that there is a civil war in Vietnam and we have decided to support one side. Unfortunately it is equally clear that the side we are supporting seems to command very little respect or affection either inside or outside Vietnam.

The government in Saigon is unstable, inefficient and corrupt. That it survives because of the support of what is virtually an occupation army of Americans has not enhanced its popularity.

It is our bitter experience, on the other hand, that a very large number of Vietnamese resent and oppose our intervention in their affairs. That we have a military force of some half million Americans, Australians and Koreans trying to pacify some of these Vietnamese opponents is some evidence of their dedication and the strength of their support among the population.

The more honest, if less attractive, reason for our intervention in Vietnam is that irrespective of the moral issues involved in the Vietnamese civil war, we have intervened to protect our interests.

Just as you Americans feel threatened by world communism, so do we Australians feel threatened by the prospect of a strong militant and unfriendly Asia. As one member of our Government put it to me "We've got to stop these —s before they get here."

It is no small thing to be willing to kill people in a remote country which has offered us no provocation merely to safeguard what we conceive to be our political interests. I believe such a policy will fail by its moral bankruptcy alone.

But it is worse than this.

Our immediate objective is to halt the progress of communism in Vietnam. Yet by our own military policies of "kill and destroy" we are creating the very conditions of social and economic chaos which communists need for their success.

At the same time we have associated the cause of anti-communism with the brutality, repression and corruption of a thoroughly discredited junta of generals.

Whatever your military advisers say, Mr President, the burning of crops, the bombing of villages, the killing of men, women and children are no way to improve a political situation.

On the wider international scene this war is doing the cause of communism very little harm.

Nor is it doing us much good.

People all over the world are tired of military solutions and power politics. They are tired of anti-communism as a substitute for commonsense. And above all they are tired of the killing.

As one of these people, and as a person having no connection or influence with any political party or organisation whatsoever, I have written this letter as a matter of personal conscience.

Friday 21st October, 1966

Yours sincerely,

GORDON BARTON

Authorised by Mr G. P. Barton, 22 MORELLA PLACE, CASTLE COVE.

The Gordon Barton advertisement in the Sydney Morning Herald on 22nd of October,1966.

Gordon and Vonnie Barton.

An opportunity arose when President Lyndon Johnson was to visit Australia, the first time an American President would come here. How to get his message to the President was the challenge to Gordon. His answer was to use the press. Gordon booked a full page advertisement in the *Sydney Morning Herald* for the day the President was to arrive in Sydney. To Gordon the price of $1742 was easily affordable. When the copy of Gordon's letter to the President arrived at the *Herald*, it was thought to be too political and so not acceptable. Gordon persevered and finally it was accepted and printed on Saturday 22nd October 1966.

Among the many people who were moved by the letter, described as one of the most incisive and heartfelt letters ever seen in print, was Ken Thomas. He went to Gordon's house and for several hours that day they discussed the matter. Gordon Barton was overwhelmed with messages of support, with phone calls, letters to his home and business, and he realised people were looking to him for some leadership in what to do next.

A federal election was due in just four weeks, on 26th November. The public response indicated an important issue was the Vietnam War and Australia's role. Gordon and Ken agreed that there should be an anti-war voice in the campaign, and an opportunity for people to vote that way. To do that a party would have to be established, registered, candidates found and only then could they campaign for votes. In such a short time it was seen as an impossible task. Garry Richardson became fully involved. Garry was a millionaire whose father, Mervyn, had invented the rotary lawnmower, then set up a factory to manufacture and sell it as the Victa.

An impossible task was a challenge to these three men, Thomas, Barton and Richardson, so they decided to go for it.

The party was named the Liberal Reform Group, as the supporters were mainly Liberal voters who disagreed with the Vietnam policy of the Liberal Government. As the campaign got going Barton sent a telegram to Harold Holt offering to withdraw the Liberal Reform candidates from the election if Holt agreed to withdraw Australian troops from Vietnam. Holt replied saying he was not interested in the *"Alice in Wonderland"* proposal.

"Where you go, we will go."—McMahon

AUSTRALIA NEEDS TRADE NOT WAR

A vote for these men IS A VOTE AGAINST WAR IN ASIA AND FOR AN INDEPENDENT AUSTRALIA

Gordon Barton, B.A., LL.B., B.Ec., *educated S.C.E.G.S. Syd. University. Chairman, IPEC Group of Companies. Former President Sydney University Liberal Club. Married with two children. Founder and leader of the Australian Reform Movement.*

Ken Thomas, B.A., B.Ec., *educated Fort St. High, Syd. University, (evening student), Former bank-clerk, station-hand, salesman, school teacher, personnel officer. Went into business with one truck in 1946 and built it into Thomas Nationwide Transport Limited, Australia's biggest transport organisation — is now Chairman and Managing Director. Married with 5 children. Co-Founder and Deputy Leader of the Australian Reform Movement.*

Paul Allsop, A.M.I.E., *Chartered Engineer. 25 years with Commonwealth Public Service. Federal and State President of Australian Council of Salaried and Professional Associations (A.C.S.P.A.) since its foundation 11 years ago.*

Peter Mason, M.Sc., Ph.D., *Fellow Inst. of Physics. Previously with C.S.I.R.O. In 1966 was appointed to Chair of Physics at Macquarie University. Married with 3 children.*

Harry Seidler, M.Arch (Harvard) Hon. F.A.I.A., A.R.A.I.A. *Won Wilkinson Award R.A.I.A. 1966-67. Visiting Lecturer and Design Critic Sydney University and University of N.S.W. Has designed many major buildings including Australia Square. Married, 1 child.*

AUSTRALIAN SENATE ELECTIONS 25 TH. NOVEMBER

VOTE AUSTRALIAN REFORM MOVEMENT

AUTHORISED BY N. GORSHENIN, 128 TRYON ROAD, EAST LINDFIELD *PRINTED BY PUBLICITY PRESS.*

The Senate election advertisement in 1967.

166

The three men worked hard gathering support, looking for candidates and raising money.

When nomination closed there were 22 Liberal Reform candidates, 12 in New South Wales seats and 10 in Victoria. The party had raised $50,000 in campaign funds in those few weeks. However the count on election day showed the three men and their supporters were ahead of public opinion. None of the candidates won their House of Representatives seats; the candidates averaged 5% of the votes cast in their electorates.

The Liberal Reform Party then reconsidered its future but decided to keep going and to formulate other policies and objectives. Barton was the 'public face' of the party and continued to gather support around the country.

A Senate election was to be held the following year in November 1967. Ken announced he was donating $20,000 to the party, and would be a candidate. The others standing for the Australian Reform Party (as it was now known) were Gordon Barton; Peter Mason, a Physics Professor; Paul Allsop, an engineer, and a distinguished architect, Harry Seidler. They were all well-known and respected men. The party contested only in New South Wales.

Ken decided that as Australia's role in the Vietnam War was the big issue, he should visit Vietnam to learn more about the country. However his passport was stamped with a message, NOT AVAILABLE FOR NORTH VIETNAM. So then there was a cat and mouse game about what that meant.

Ken asked the question, "Does that mean the Australian Government specifically prohibits Australians from going there, or does it mean that the government is merely giving a travel warning?"

As usual Ken went right to the top and sent a telegram to Prime Minister Harold Holt, requesting an "Urgent Extension" of his passport to cover travel to North Vietnam. Holt passed the matter to Immigration Minister Billy Sneddon. Ken had to make phone calls to Sneddon's staff before Sneddon finally replied that, "The government announced in May 1965 that passports would not be made valid for North Vietnam, and it is not considered appropriate to vary that rule at this stage."

Ken replied that he wanted to go because he was a candidate for the Senate election, and wanted to gather some facts "I am not a communist," Ken said, "and I would like a special exemption. If that cannot be done, would I be acting illegally if I went to North Vietnam?" Finally he got an answer: "Travel to a country for which a passport is not valid does not constitute an offence in Australian law." However, it was only two days before he had planned to depart that he had the answer.

Ken wrote a 10 page report after his trip. He set out his objectives of the trip.

1. Educate myself on the facts at first hand.

2. See if this would change my preconceptions that Australia should withdraw her forces.

3. See if I could make any useful, practical proposals.

Ken was not impressed with Saigon, capital of South Vietnam and described it as being an abomination. He saw it as a *"tropical slum, uncollected garbage everywhere, but no signs of hunger or malnutrition."* He found that the economic effects of the American invasion were disastrous. The money paid to the South Vietnamese soldiers was very low, and they were worse off than the peasants. The country had to import over three-quarters of the rice needed, when before the war, rice had been exported.

Ken said that women were being elected to local government positions and that over half of administrative positions in South Vietnam were held by women. The Ho Chi Minh Communist Government was popular with the South Vietnamese, and the government would start rebuilding Roman Catholic churches that were bombed by the US Airforce. *"Clearly, the American persecution is creating an invincible solidarity where all differences are submerged in the nationalist cause,"* Ken concluded.

The presence of 2500 men, of PHILCAG, the Philippines Civil Aid Group really impressed Ken. These men were not there to fight, but to help Vietnamese agriculture and the economy with new varieties of rice and teaching the farmers about its cultivation. This had the potential to increase the rice harvest 15-fold. There were other farming techniques and some civil reconstruction also being done by PHILCAG. They even arranged musicians to offer entertainment to lift the morale of the people.

Ken was enthusiastic about this sort of help, and talked about how it should be the model for Australia's role in Vietnam. He developed a plan which could become the policy for the Australian Reform Movement. The idea was Australian volunteers would go to North Vietnam and give civil aid in three fields: agriculture, medical and education. These volunteers would need to be able to speak the language, work at requested tasks only, and would need physical protection.

Although he had wanted to go to Hanoi, capital of North Vietnam, Ken did not get there. Instead he went to Phnom Penh, capital of Cambodia, and discussed his plan with the Senior Counsellor of the North Vietnam Embassy.

While he aroused interest, Ken came away thinking that the Vietnamese really wanted to be left alone to run their country, without the "white man."

Ken realised that the Vietnamese had had many years of foreign occupation. Originally it was the French, and they fled when the Japanese arrived. Then after the Second World War, the French wanted to come back, which resulted in a war in 1954 when the Vietnamese resisted them. Then the United States wanted to keep the Chinese out and reinstall the French. All this was an interference for a peaceful, hard-working people wanting a happy life.

Back in Australia the Senate polling day was 25th November 1967. However, the Australian Reform team were not successful; Gordon Barton, at the top of the ticket, won only 39,000 votes. The number needed to win a New South Wales Senate Seat was over 300,000.

Ken then proposed that the name of the party be changed again, this time to the Australian Freedom Party.

Ken's two younger sons, Gavin and Andrew, were pupils at North Sydney Boys High School, and the Annual Speech Day in December 1967 was addressed by Hon. John Waddy, DFC, a distinguished World War Two fighter pilot, who then became a Liberal MLA in the New South Wales Parliament. Waddy told the boys that while they would go separate ways in their careers some of them were likely to be called up for national service. "I would not worry about this," he said.

Ken Thomas had arrived late for the event and was at the rear of the hall, while his family were seated near the front. When Waddy mentioned National Service, Ken called out, "Why don't you go?" Waddy ignored the heckler and went on to say, "Don't look at National Service as a chore. Look on it as a privilege. Many more young Australians are being killed in road accidents than are being killed in Vietnam." Waddy said he had left a young son at home to serve five years in the RAAF.

When John Waddy had finished, the chairman apologised to him for Ken's interjection. This stirred Ken, who jumped up and called out, "I challenge Mr Waddy to debate the issue in public at any time and at any place." The crowd was in uproar. Anne, Ken's wife, was mortified, and the chairman tried to bring order, saying, "Sit down Mr Thomas, this is not the place for that sort of talk."

Two things about these remarks got under Ken's skin. The first was Waddy's support of the Vietnam War. The second was the implication that a high road toll was acceptable and so justified the killing of young men. Road safety was another of Ken's passions. Ken accosted John Waddy outside as he went to his car, and repeated the challenge. Waddy said, "I will not debate with you. The Australian public gave their answer to your views at the Senate election."

The encounter made headlines in the press. *The Sydney Morning Herald* had it on the front page and the *Daily Telegraph* printed a repeat of the challenge of a debate.

Ken loved it all as he enjoyed a stoush of minds, so he pushed the issue. Waddy continued to refuse the challenge. An old school friend from Fort Street High, Ken Gee, a barrister and Secretary of the Friends of Vietnam movement, who opposed Ho Chi Minh because he was a communist, got in touch with Ken and offered a debate. The press gave it plenty of space and Ken paid for a newspaper advertisement, inviting attendance at the meeting.

On Wednesday 13th December 1967, the Sydney University Theatre was packed with 600 people to hear the contest. Mr Justice Dovey had agreed to be Chairman. Ken Thomas opened by saying that he agreed with Ken Gee that they were there to air their differences. Ken Thomas gave a very good and detailed account of Vietnam and the problems of the people. The information he had collected on his trip was thoroughly aired; he maintained that the Unites States had no business being involved, and nor had Australia.

Although as a barrister Ken Gee was expected to be a better debater, Ken Thomas won a lot of support. Messages came in from people all over Australia, congratulating him on the stand he was making and the demonstration of free speech.

Gordon Barton continued with the Australia Party but the heat went out of the Vietnam issue as the Whitlam led Labor Party gained popularity. The withdrawal from Vietnam was a promise made by Whitlam, and implemented after Labor won government in December 1972.

In June 1969, Ken set up an office in Pitt Street, Sydney to form the Australian Peace Institute. It was to be a permanent focal point for peace information and research. Ken wanted peace to be a respectable cause and not a front for 'left wing loonys'. It would support compulsory military training for home defence. While Ken shared this plan with other respected and prominent citizens it did not win enough support to proceed.

Meanwhile Ken continued to campaign against conscription, and became a leader of the Anti-Conscription Group who advised young men not to register for national service, as they were required to do at age 18. In November 1969 Ken was summoned to court for his role in this group.

There was another aspect relating to politics that aroused Ken, and that was compulsory voting. For some years he took the view that people should be free to decline to vote. When he went to the polling booth, he would have his name marked off, collect the ballot paper, put it in his pocket and walk out. The attendant staff got really flustered but could do nothing about it. In one election he wrote to the returning officer some weeks beforehand and said that he would not be casting a vote. He advised the time he would be at the booth to be marked off. On the day he did his usual, collected the paper and walked out, and nothing happened.

In the last election of his lifetime, he did not go to the booth; but he did show his colours.

In January 1996, Dick Smith, the well-known Australian entrepreneur, decided to organise a "Time To Change" campaign. Dick wrote to Ken and said that after 13 years Australia should change from a Labor to a Liberal Government. Dick was looking for support from famous Australians to join him in calling for this change. Ken was one of 19 who accepted this invitation. Dick Smith paid for newspaper advertisements listing these supporters and urging votes for the Liberal Party. After the election, Ken received a thank you note for his support from John Howard, the new prime minister.

John Howard was no doubt unaware that despite the advertisement, Ken had not voted for his Liberal candidate. As usual Ken did not vote, so was sent a please explain letter. He wrote a four page letter in reply and out-lined his reasons in great detail. There were several paragraphs on each of his five objections.

1. None of the candidates was fit for a place in the parliament.

2. That one of the ballot papers was for the Senate, and he believed that the Senate should be abolished.

3. He felt he was entitled to abstain from voting, as this is a right of the members in parliament.

4. For the Electoral Commission to say voting is compulsory was wrong, as all that was compulsory was having the name marked off.

5. Compulsory voting meant that it herded the not interested and the ill-informed voters to the poll, and they swamped the intelligent vote.

For these reasons his letter said he would not pay the $20 fine imposed. Six months later Ken was summoned to court. Ken did not appear so was fined $50 plus $51 costs, payable within three months.

Ken loved a fight and a chance to air his views, a champion of free speech. Despite his interest in political matters at no stage did Ken join the Liberal Party or the Labor Party.

He did join the Australian Democrat Party. In April 1980 Ken was asked to speak at a meeting of the democrats in Sydney. He decided on the night to join the party, paid his $18 subscription, and was given some literature on the democrats' policies to take home. Within a week he decided that he could not accept the party policy on regionalism. Consequently he promptly resigned.

Column 8 in the *Sydney Morning Herald* heard about that, and wrote that the party had lost a millionaire.

The next day, they ran a postscript sent in by Ken: *"I am much obliged to the Herald for making me a millionaire. Knowing your reputation for factual reporting, I would be happy to receive your cheque for $999,000 to establish me in the condition you reported yesterday."*

THE TAKEOVER
OF ALLTRANS

Ken Thomas and Peter Abeles had been in a business relationship since 1964 when they had agreed to establish Comet as an overnight express carrier. Comet had done well and was making a profit, and both partners were pleased about that.

It had also allowed Ken and Peter to get to know each other and be aware of the skills each had. There had been rumours about further joint ventures but Ken had denied that speculation.

On 23rd August 1966 Ken sent a memo to his senior executives to tell them that Peter Abeles had just returned from abroad and the first thing he did was to call on Ken and sit down and talk about special arrangements between TNT and Alltrans. He said, "At Managing Director level, Mr Abeles and I confer with each other a good deal about mutual problems and pool our ideas, plans and even what might be called trade secrets."

They had discussed the matter of a sharing of terminals in some places, and Perth was particularly on their minds. They also pledged that there would

Peter Abeles.

be no price cutting or taking of each other's customers. They would go even further than required by the NFFA (National Freight Forwarders Association) to which they both belonged. They would in future quote over the transport price scale (set by the NFFA) to protect each other. They would even inform each other of any complaints heard from customers about the service of the other. Ken said in the final paragraph, *"No deviation from the above may occur without specific references to myself and Mr Abeles."*

Obviously there was mutual respect and trust between them.

It was late in 1966, that they discussed a complete merger. TNT was much larger than Alltrans so the plan evolved that TNT would buy Alltrans and add it to the TNT stable.

They each tabled their figures. TNT had a capital value with shareholders, funds of $4.9 million. Alltrans shareholder funds were $1 million, Alltrans had an earning rate a little higher than TNT, and TNT had a higher asset backing of each share.

It was agreed that the price for TNT to pay for the Alltrans business was $1 million. However, this was to be achieved by the exchange of a TNT share for an Alltrans share. TNT had a value of 50 cents par share, and being a listed public company the shares were quoted on the stock exchange, and were currently trading there at $1.33.

Alltrans was not a public company so was not listed on the exchange; the tightly held shares had a par value of $1. Peter Abeles owned 29.8%, his partner and fellow executive George Rockey had 29.8%; 5.5% were owned by Alltrans staff, and the biggest shareholder was another company, William Baird and Company Ltd, with 35%. There were 2.4 million shares altogether.

Bairds was a United Kingdom company which had been very impressed with Alltrans and had bought the shares as an investment. When the directors of Bairds heard of the TNT proposal they were reluctant to sell as they wanted to stay as a shareholder. Actually their initial reaction was a desire to buy another 25% of the Alltrans shares, which could only have come from Abeles or Rockey. Both men declined to sell to Bairds, as that would give them too little equity in TNT. When Bairds became involved with Alltrans it had been agreed that if they wanted to sell the shares they had to sell the lot, or nothing. Consequently Bairds shares could be sold to TNT, or privately to another investor wanting to obtain TNT shares.

On 7th April 1967, Ken wrote a formal letter to Peter Abeles to make an offer, in these terms.

TNT makes this proposal to Alltrans shareholders:

1. In respect to holdings by William Baird & Co Ltd., one TNT 50 cents fully paid share for each fully paid one dollar share in Alltrans.

OR

$1.33 cash for each fully paid one dollar share in Alltrans.

2. In respect to holdings by other shareholders, one TNT share of 50 cents, fully paid, for each one dollar share in Alltrans.

OR

One TNT share of 50 cents fully paid, plus $1.33 for every two fully paid one dollar Alltrans shares.

There were a number of conditions, and the major one was that Peter Abeles and George Rockey would stay on, and were restricted in working for any other transport company in the years ahead.

On 27th April, Ken as Chairman of TNT wrote to the Secretary of the Sydney Stock Exchange to formally advise the market of the offer.

Ken had also written a press release which was circulated that day. It read:

TNT MERGER WITH ALLTRANS GROUP

The close association that has existed between TNT and Alltrans has now developed into a full merger.

Hitherto both companies have jointly owned Comet Overnight Express Pty Ltd, and the success of this venture has led them to contemplate further enterprises in partnership. It is firmly intended that both TNT and Alltrans will continue to trade as separate organisations. There will be no merging of staff, and both transport services will continue to operate as at present without any change in name or in methods of control. Independent boards will function in both operating companies.

Both groups have a common feature, in that the founders of both organisations are still taking an active part in their business. TNT was founded in 1946 by K.W.Thomas (the present managing director): The Alltrans Group was founded in 1950 by Messrs E.H.P Abeles (the present managing director) and G. Rockey.

The pattern of the future development of TNT as a listed company on the stock exchange is now clear. It is emerging as the holding company for a large group of wholly owned or part owned subsidiaries throughout Australia and New Zealand, notably the parent company itself with 25 companies operating under the TNT flag, Rudders Ltd (Customs and Shipping); the Alltrans Group, Australia and New Zealand wide; Wood Transport (Gold Coast); Freight Transfer company; P.E.Power (Wagga); Comet Overnight

Express; Seatons Transport and a number of smaller enterprises. This form of organisation closely follows the example of the highly successful Transport Development Group of Great Britain (who are substantial shareholders in TNT), but in their case the parent company does not trade. A complete parallel would exist if TNT should change its name as the listed company but retained its dynamic title for trading purposes.

COST REDUCTIONS

The merger with Alltrans is seen as an intelligent and practical scheme for ideal transport organisation. The industry is subject to extremely fine profit margins. TNT's last annual report shows a profit per revenue dollar of only 3.6 cents. Interstate transport prices are now in fact lower than they were 20 years ago, despite the fact that costs have more than doubled in that period. The best way to bridge the gap is by savings in terminal and equipment cost, and by electronic data processing. The economics of the industry will no longer permit a large number of small operators to maintain small terminals in all capital cities, much less in provincial centres. On the other hand, the problem is to organise the service so that each individual customer continues to get personal attention for his separate needs. The best of both worlds should therefore result from this grouping whereby several companies share facilities but continue to operate as completely separate entities.

CONTAINERISATION

On a national and international level, containerisation is moving ahead very vigorously. Before this merger TNT and Alltrans had been jointly developing their plans for the future on containers and during the next few years tremendous savings must be made through this rationalisation. It is expected that the proper usage of containers in Australia, across the Tasman and New Zealand and on the international level, will open up excellent and profitable possibilities for the merged group.

TERMINAL SAVINGS

Economies will come from the joint use of terminals and facilities in outports where TNT is already well established with excellent terminals, some of which are not fully developed. For example, in North Queensland TNT have four terminals, and a further three in Tasmania where space and facilities can be made for Alltrans to become established at the same sites. Similarly in Perth, Alltrans will sell its 12-acre holding at Kewdale marshalling yards and will switch its proposed railhead terminal and warehouse to spare land held by TNT where rail tracks and access yards are already provided. The same sort of terminal sharing will occur in Canberra, Newcastle and Wollongong where TNT has extensive properties. TNT has a plan to establish 50 branches, of which 31 already exist, and these will serve 86% of the Australian population. Each of these branches in the provincial centres will incorporate facilities for joint operation with Alltrans, in much the same way as airline companies share terminals in smaller centres.

NEW ZEALAND

The Alltrans group has pioneered the development of Australian freight forwarding methods throughout New Zealand, where they are now successfully established—with branches and agencies in all major centres. This will enable the TNT network to offer, with the advent of roll-on roll-off ships, during the next few years—parallel with Alltrans—door-to-door service from all points in Australia to any point in New Zealand.

TRAVEL

The Alltrans group owns the nucleus of a future international travel organisation, with a travel bureau in Angel Place, Sydney, and two offices in Los Angeles, USA. We hope to benefit from the expected tourist explosion in the late 1960s and 1970s.

FINANCIAL CONTROL

At present both TNT and Alltrans operate separate computers. Rationalisation in this section will certainly show savings in the overall group.

PROSPECTS

The merger will make a significant increase in the profits of TNT, the listed company. Directors expect that the earning rate will exceed 22% on average capital during this financial year and that this will rise to over 23% on the expanded capital next year, provided the general economy shows no decline. TNT has an annual revenue of approximately $30 million, and Alltrans is about $15 million, making the combined group with a $45 million annual turnover the largest transport organisation in Australasia.

K.W. Thomas, Managing Director, TNT

E.H.P. Abeles, Managing Director, Alltrans

The shares in Alltrans were so tightly held that once Bairds had agreed on the sale of its shares there was no problem, and the takeover could proceed.

One of the first questions for study was the use of computers. Alltrans were further advanced with this new tool than TNT, but the systems both companies had were to be used, so Ken and Peter asked some of their respective staff to study how this could best be done.

The big question was the way to structure the directors and senior management. The Alltrans company would continue as an operating company, but some Alltrans directors would sit on the TNT board. Then TNT had an operating board of management below the main board.

Peter Abeles advised Ken that he and Frederick Millar would be the Alltrans appointees to the TNT board.

While Ken and Peter had got along well, there were differences in their makeup and style.

Peter was a man who liked to rub shoulders with the well known to improve his contacts and seek business opportunities. In 1954, just four years after starting Alltrans, Peter and George Rockey had managed to meet Sir William McKell, a former Labor Premier of NSW, and later, Governor-General of Australia from 1949 to 1953.

Peter cultivated this relationship and within a few months of meeting him, invited Sir William to be Chairman of the Alltrans Board. This gave Alltrans a prestige and profile, and was typical of the way Abeles operated. He also established friendly relationships with other politicians, both Labor and Liberal, and donated money to both parties.

Peter was to develop a strong friendship with Bob Hawke. Peter had brought this about by contacting Bob, then a staff member of the ACTU (Australian

Council of Trade Unions) and asking to talk about unions. Bob agreed to see Peter and the relationship developed from that meeting. Peter had later bought a house in Victoria Rd, Bellevue Hill—a very prestigious address.

That was a complete contrast to Ken Thomas, who had no time for such social climbing.

The other new TNT director, Frederick Millar, was a lawyer who at age 30 became a partner in Allen Allen and Hemsley. This was a high profile Sydney law firm that did a lot of commercial legal work for major companies.

Fred was an Albury boy; he left school at 15, and was a junior public service clerk before he joined the army and became a signalman during the war, studying law in his spare time. He had a schoolboy sense of humour, and a habit of calling others 'cocko'. One of his contemporaries described him as "rough as bags, very able, ingenious and resourceful in the wretched field of taxation law."

Peter Abeles had wanted some legal work done, so he went to a leading firm, met and got to know Fred, and a friendship developed. From this Peter had invited Fred to be a director of Alltrans. Fred collected directorships and chairmanships as that proved a good way to attract legal work. At one stage Fred was on the board of 44 companies and was killing himself with overwork. He specialised in company takeovers and was a true commercial lawyer. He once wrote a one and a half page letter to Kerry Packer, containing some legal advice, and charged him £8000. Kerry objected, but paid the bill.

These two new directors on the TNT board would make a difference, as Ken would find out.

From Ken's point of view the major advantage was that a problem he had been wrestling with was solved. Ken knew the importance of succession planning. Some time previously he had decided that retirement at age 58 would be a good idea, and that would mean 1971. However, he needed to have someone who he was sure of to take over, and up to then it was a question of who? He had appointed as general manager an Englishman, by the name of Price, a few years previously with that intention, but he had not fitted in so that had not worked.

Part of the attraction of Alltrans was that Peter Abeles was 11 years younger than Ken, and there was Ross Cribb.

Ross was a young ANZ bank teller when Ken met him in 1954, and was impressed with his style and manner. Ross was also a country boy, born in Grafton in 1931, and Ken liked country people. Being an ethical man, Ken spoke to the bank manager about Ross and received his approval and support in offering Ross a job at K.W. Thomas. Of course Ken was smart enough to realise that poaching the staff was not a good way to stay on good terms with the bank manager, so he carefully waited for the manager to suggest to Ross that he meet Ken for an interview. That led to Ross having seven years training in transport before he left to work for himself in a small transport company. In 1962 Peter Abeles bought that company and Ross, being part of the package, went to Alltrans. Ken Thomas was keen to get Ross back into his company.

Geoff Hammond, the first accountant, was phasing himself out. He had been Ken's friend, supporter and loyal fellow director for over 20 years, since the first truck. Ken and Geoff still got on well, regularly visited each other's homes, the Hammonds still lived in Melbourne, and their families were friends.

Geoff's daughter Christine remembers Ken to be handsome, charming and quite a ladies' man.

Geoff understood and admired Ken's political activities, but did not take a part in the anti-Vietnam war campaign. Geoff was not impressed with Peter Abeles, and did not like him. Geoff still had his respect for Ken, but felt it was time to step down. He had made enough money so he quietly slipped into the background. Geoff had built himself a yacht, and named it 'Mia Mia' so he now wanted to do more sailing, including a trip to New Guinea. He particularly planned to revisit and show his family the battle areas and war cemeteries where he served in the war. He remained living in Melbourne until the 1990s. Geoff died on the Gold Coast in 2005.

Ken Smith, who had joined the business as the operations manager, had also stood down from his full time executive responsibilities. However, he maintained his connection with the business as a part-time director. In this role he advised and did some overseas travel to watch transport developments in other countries. The two Kens had a few differences of opinion, so Ken Smith used the money he had made to buy a 600-acre dairy farm at Mulgoa, west of Sydney. The farm was large and in the Milk Zone so was quite profitable, which allowed him to employ staff to do the milking, and Ken Smith could still maintain the home at Castlecrag as a neighbour of Ken Thomas. Ken Smith then had time to be involved in dairy farmer politics and become Vice President of the Milk Zone Dairyman's Association. Ken Smith died in October 2011 at age 95.

With the Alltrans acquisition, there had to be some reconstruction of the management.

Ken Thomas formed a head office group, with Peter Abeles, Ross Cribb and four other executives, Bill Martin, Keith Stewart, Neville Grace and Fred Golan. Ken was to be the managing director, and Peter the chief executive.

Ken sent a memo to his executives and directors in which he said that Alltrans makes a great deal more profit per revenue dollar, and per tangible asset dollar than TNT. He said that he thought that was because of superior organisation which can only be emulated by adopting the Alltrans EDP system.

The memo went on; *"You will see from the above that there will be a lot of changes. Do not resist them, because change is vitality. The objective is to increase TNT's profit by 75% next year... I am confident that working together we will eventually re-establish TNT on an earning rate of 15% to shareholders funds."*

Following the Cargo Distributors take over, the Transport Development Group in the UK had about a quarter of the TNT shares issued.

There was a director on the board representing their interest. The concern they had was the future management of the company, so they wanted Ken to have a written contract with TNT, and to tie himself to the managing director's position for some years ahead. Ken Thomas was not keen on that idea, and there was considerable correspondence with London, and face-to-face meetings. Ken was looking forward to getting out but did not want to commit himself as to when.

In January 1966 Ken reduced his own annual salary to £4,500 ($9,000), on the idea that he would work only three-quarters of the time for TNT, and the balance would be spent on his other interests. This was the time that Ken was watching the Vietnam War closely, and being active and outspoken about Australia's involvement. However, in June he had to say that the part-time plan did not work, and he was still working full time for TNT, so increased his own salary to $15,000 per year.

When Peter Abeles came onto the payroll his salary was set at $40,000, and Ken's was increased to $20,000 per year.

1967 was also the year that Ken tackled the North Queensland transport need. Ken had been interested in that part of Australia for years, and realised the geography needed a special transport response. It is 1700 km, a considerable distance, from Brisbane to Cairns. Along the way there are some important towns and cities that were reasonably large and growing so had freight needs from the interstate capital cities. Until then these places had been served by ships, but as the shipping services declined a new need emerged. Rail was an option, but with break of gauge at Brisbane, this meant handling and delay. Ken decided to provide a service by road from Sydney and Melbourne.

In typical Ken Thomas style he decided to do the job properly. Firstly he gave it a name, North Queensland Express Pty Ltd (NQX), and registered it as a separate company. Then there was a manager and staff appointed, and the trucks were sign-written. The service was from each of Sydney and Melbourne direct to North Queensland, and with drops at as few as possible of the destination towns. It was not practicable to depart daily, so freight was accumulated during the week and despatched on Friday. This way delivery was possible early in the following week. The service was a success and grew to become a major carrier for this traffic.

The secret of the success was having the volume to provide more frequent despatches and concentrated delivery points. A competitor with many consignments might have to start deliveries as far south as Maryborough, so

A skeletal trailer built to carry containers.

further north deliveries were delayed, and the truck was only part loaded for a considerable distance: not the way to make money.

After the integration of the Cargo Distributor companies, then some other smaller companies—Cousins, Nobles, Mutual Transport, Dawson and Rowe, and then the Alltrans group into TNT—there were some impressive statistics. The features and advantages Ken wrote about at the time of the buyout were reflected on the scoreboard early in 1968.

The TNT company now had over 100 subsidiaries, 4000 employees, 3000 vehicles (including full-time owner/driver sub-contractors), 1000 other pieces of equipment, 75 terminals in Australia and 17 branches in New Zealand.

Annual turn-over was about $50 million; 95% in Australia, and 5% in New Zealand. The company handled 70,000 consignments each week, weighing about 60,000 tons.

It is not easy to compare the sizes of transport companies as they each have a different work pattern so the measure to fairly assess them is hard to find.

For example, Mayne Nickless was then very big in carrying money in armoured cars. That meant three men in each vehicle, carrying very little weight a short distance. Mayne Nickless was a service for which a much higher charge was made than the TNT services by comparing ton/miles. TNT did 90% of its carrying from one state to another, and the majority of that by rail. TNT's freight costs paid to all the railway systems was up to about $14 million per year.

A way to measure them is hard to find. However it can confidently be said that two years earlier Mayne Nickless had been Australia's largest carrier, but TNT had now overtaken them and was double the size of Mayne Nickless. As Mayne Nickless were established 60 years earlier than TNT they had a big start.

The Mascot terminal that Ken designed and had built only 11 years previously, then extended, was now the busiest and most elaborate in Australia. At any one time it could handle 26 long distance semi-trailers and 40 to 50 smaller trucks and vans for pick-ups and deliveries. It handled well over 1000 tons per day, and they were only the smaller and lighter consignments. Alltrans had an office and depot in Burrows Road, only a couple of kilometres away, so that was used by some operations.

The key to success is management. Large size becomes a liability if the management is not up to the task. Ken was at the centre of this as he had developed the management system as the company grew.

There were 16 major subsidiaries in the TNT group, trading autonomously, headed by a general manager reporting weekly to head office. The figures from these reports were fed into a computer working 16 hours a day. The formula that Ken developed of head office setting a uniform method of control and recording, together with the decentralised operating companies finding and moving the freight, was a success.

Revenue from trading had about quadrupled in the five years from 1963 to 1968. Capital employed or total assets had gone from $5,518,000 to $25,987,000 in the same period. Earnings to capital had also gone up to 22.7% in 1968.

In 1968, Ken and his executives reviewed their decision to use Flexitainers and Flexiflats as their rail vehicles. There were a number of problems. The major one was there had to be specialised and dedicated equipment ready as and where needed. The load balance had to be just right, the need to disconnect electric and brake hoses, then tyre scrub, and the high maintenance on the road vehicles were all problems. Consequently they decided to rely on crane transfers from road to rail. The new system would use containers of varying lengths. There were rail flatcars available, and TNT staff designed a skeletal road trailer, which could be hauled by any prime mover to carry the containers. Another advantage was that loading operation of about five minutes by one man was quicker.

TNT built their own cranes at railway yards to transfer containers.

December 1968 saw the first issue of 'Freight Notes,' a company staff magazine.

The title was suggested by two staff members, as freight notes was the paper system started back in 1948 to minimise the inevitable paper war of the growing business. Ken Thomas and Geoff Hammond had led the industry with this simpler system.

In 'Freight Notes', Ken very proudly announced the new superannuation scheme that the board had approved for all employees. This was the latest step in the policy which Ken had expressed back in 1963. He said then:

"The objective of TNT is to provide the best transport service in Australia, and this is being achieved by developing the best transport staff in Australia."

Ken wanted to develop each staff member to their maximum capacity and reward them accordingly. Updating and improving their retirement benefits was very important to Ken.

The new superannuation scheme provided for a contribution of 4% of wages by an employee, and the company would contribute 6%. It was a defined benefit scheme, which was quite courageous as the company promised the retirement benefit, and would have to increase the employer contribution if the investments did not make enough money. Ken said it was the most liberal in the transport industry, and he did not know of such a generous scheme anywhere else. The scheme would cost the company $250,000 in the first year.

In 1968 such a generous company contribution to ALL employees was way ahead of its time. It was only in the 1990s that such a contribution was required of employers by industrial awards, or by government statute.

The magazine also told of the building and opening in November 1968 of a new cold store at Chullora in Sydney for TNT Refrigeration. Ken Thomas had invited the Hon. Doug Anthony, then Deputy Prime Minister and Federal Minister for Primary Industry to inspect and open the new building. It was the largest single-level commercial cold store in New South Wales, and its major use was to be for meat awaiting shipment to the USA. The building contained 575,000 cubic feet of cold store space.

Top: *A refrigerated truck loads at the cold store at Chullora, Sydney.*

Bottom: *Hon. Doug Anthony opens the new cold store.*

TNT had been in the refrigerated transport business since 1964 when they bought Armstrong Refrigerated Freighters and revamped the cold store/ refrigerated transport business. They bought a fleet of refrigerated volume vans and refrigerated containers for road, rail and sea. Very quickly they were handling about 1500 different types of cargo that had to be kept cold or frozen. There were Australian products for local markets and exports, as well as imports. A good deal of technical skill was needed to design and build these refrigerators that would provide reliable cold transport at a set temperature over long distances.

On 27th November 1968, the first standard gauge train with the wagons going right through to Perth left Sydney. As the standard gauge was not then operative between Broken Hill and Port Pirie, the rail wagons went via Melbourne and were given bogie changes at Melbourne and Port Pirie. The important thing was the cargo loaded in Sydney was not touched, or the rail wagon unlocked until the 3250km trip was completed at the Perth suburb of Kewdale. TNT had built a $750,000 multi-purpose terminal at Kewdale as the centre for its Western Australia operations.

Ken gave another indication of his character in the 1970 annual report, when he wrote: *"The results of our year's work are not measured in dollars alone. Our contribution to the quality of life is another important test, but that is hard to assess. One of our concerns at TNT is with road safety and we aim to make some contributions in this area. Our report tells of the TNT trains each having the effect of taking 130 semi-trailers off the Hume Highway. When we double the train volume there will be 260 semi-trailers displaced...this is good for safety, and for national transport economics."*

The report told shareholders that the company had stepped into shipping, with the purchase of a portion of Bulkships Ltd .

Bulkships was a company owned in equal shares by Adelaide Steamships and McIlwraith McEachern. They owned and operated four modern bulk ore carriers, three cellular container ships and several other ships serving Australian ports. The company also had an interest in Seatainer Terminals. TNT had bought a third of the shares of Bulkships, and so was well involved in operating sea transport.

1969 saw a major development with services to New Zealand. Alltrans had been established in New Zealand for five years and had built a network of branches there. It made sense that the Australian and New Zealand branches be linked with an efficient and reliable shipping service.

This was accomplished when the Union Steam Ship Company introduced two new ships: the *Maheno* and the *Marama*. They were roll-on, roll-off, bigger and faster than others on the trans-Tasman service. Each vessel could carry 4000 tons on three decks. General and refrigerated 16ft containers were used, and there were stalls for livestock. They were scheduled to each do a fortnightly run and serve Sydney, Melbourne, Auckland, Wellington and Lyttelton.

The *Financial Review* of 23rd June 1970 gave a detailed account of the TNT trains, which it said was the first of its kind in Australia, and believed to be first in the world. The service started on 8th June, under an agreement TNT, the largest Australian road rail transport group, had made with the New South Wales and Victorian railways.

The *Financial Review* said: *"The schedule called for freight expresses exclusively for TNT, every night, except Sundays, each way between Sydney and Melbourne. The train leaves the Cooks River, Sydney rail yard at 7.38pm, and arrives in Melbourne at 12.29pm the next day. Northbound the train leaves*

Melbourne at 6.34pm each day arriving in Sydney at 11.57am. The distance of 597 miles is covered in 17 hours. The trains carry a net load of 350 tons of freight, equivalent to 23 semi-trailer loads. This was 250,000 tons of cargo each year.

TNT has signed a contract to permanently hire 42 bogie flatcars on a fixed annual rent. It is up to TNT to maximise their use. Each flatcar carries two BC type containers, specially designed for rail traffic by company engineering staff. The railways supply two diesel electric locos and crew."

To handle this volume of cargo, Ken had arranged the long-term lease of railway land in both Sydney and Melbourne to build a new terminal in each city at a cost of $800,000 each. To quickly move the containers, 27-ton capacity overhead cranes were included. A container transfer took only four minutes, and 800 tons of cargo was being handled in less than two hours.

This service was proving so effective, Ken had plans for extending it to Adelaide and Brisbane, and then to Perth.

Mr Ted Woods, a retired New South Wales Railways executive, told Ken Thomas that as the rolling stock was doing 3500 miles a week it was a world record for rail vehicles carrying general cargo.

Looking back it is very apparent that Ken's genius was the perception that rail transport could be both very efficient and profitable. Without doubt Ken's vision led the way, not only in Australia, but also overseas.

"RAIL FREIGHT HANDLED BY TRANSPORT COMPANIES, BETWEEN SYDNEY, MELBOURNE AND BRISBANE HAD RISEN FROM 7,000 TONS IN 1950, TO 700,000 TONS IN 1970."

—KEN THOMAS

LIFE WITH ALLTRANS

Ken Thomas and Peter Abeles had known each other for several years, but now they had to 'live together'. They were both strong men, accustomed to being in charge and making decisions, so making compromises to arrive at a joint decision had its hazards.

Joy Annard, Peter's secretary for 40 years, remembers that the two men had a good relationship and respected each other. Peter was dedicated to his job, was a natural leader, and inspired his employees. Joy saw that Peter was a generous man and gave big sums to needy people and causes. Peter was particularly passionate about cancer research, and his efforts led to the establishment of the Cancer Research Foundation. He gave generously and chaired the foundation.

Peter Abeles was elevated to the position of Joint Managing Director of TNT and Ross Cribb became general manager. Ken was chairman of the board and joint managing director and so not caught up with the day to-day problems. He was able as a well-known, successful and respected business man to do other things, and had status as he still led the company. Later Ken dropped

The Kwikasair Kenworths were known as 'grey ghosts'.

the joint managing director title and was satisfied with being chairman. This standing back allowed him to get a better view of the overall company and its place in Australian business.

Ken had a great deal of confidence in, and respect for, Ross Cribb, and so was able to leave the day-to-day management to Ross. Physically, Ross was a short man, so earned the nickname of the 'Angry Ant'. However, the managers who reported to Ross also found that the Ant was only angry when their weekly reports were late, or worse, contained figures less than the targets Ross had given them.

In October 1968, TNT bought Kwikasair. This was the interstate overnight carrier on which Comet had been modelled, and both companies were doing well. There was no intention of merging them; Comet and Kwikasair ran separately, competing with each other, but there was no undercutting of rates. By setting them up as competitors, the executives and staff of each company worked hard to beat the others. The public did not realise the connection. This tactic was a favourite of Ken Thomas, and it worked well. The two companies did not overlap everywhere. Kwikasair specialised in servicing the capital cities, where most of the volume was. Comet gave a wider service to smaller centres, as well as the capitals. For Tasmania, Comet had a Bristol Freight plane to run from Melbourne to the island cities each night.

Kwikasair were well known along the highways for their 'grey ghosts'. That was the nickname given to their Kenworth trucks. TNT ordered 20 of these: 14 for Kwikasair, and six for Comet. Kenworth had been building trucks in the USA for many years and had just opened a factory in Australia, so the new trucks could be customised to TNT specifications. That meant a choice of engines, gear boxes, and even differentials. The trucks had to be fast to keep a tight schedule, and were a cab over, rigid bogie pantechnicon painted grey. Other truck drivers chugging along the highway found the 'grey ghosts' would suddenly appear behind them, and then at the first opportunity, overtake and disappear into the dark.

TNT found they were having problems and frequent blowouts with the front tyres of the Kenworths. The tyres were Michelins, made in France, so Michelin sent two tyre engineers to Australia to look at the operating conditions. This resulted in a new steering tyre being designed and made for this work.

The Kwikasair trucks were driven by experienced responsible drivers on a strict timetable. Drivers changed at Yass on the Hume Highway, and at Yass and Hay for Sydney-Adelaide trips. On the New England Highway there was a driver change at Murrurundi and another at Glen Innes. The drivers were well paid, the trucks were comfortable and performed well so men were very willing to drive the 'grey ghosts'.

Top: The first train to Perth with no cargo transhipment.

Bottom: The new TNT terminal in Perth.

Early in 1969, another step of Ken Thomas's dreams came true with the establishment of a branch in Port Hedland in the north-west of Western Australia. The miners had found iron ore in the Pilbara, and big things were happening. There were no rail lines from the south, and the shipping service was spasmodic, so there was a demand for road transport, and TNT was in on the ground floor. Some TNT trucks took the coastal route, and others served inland towns. By both routes it was about 1800km from Perth to Port Hedland, normally hot to very hot, and a gravel road most of the way. Although the TNT branch was at Port Hedland there were trucks going as far as Kununurra.

The experience with taking general cargo to Western Australia's north-west made TNT aware that there was a need for an express service. The scattered towns and mining camps had patchy air services, but no reliable schedule for air freight. The Comet and Kwikasair managers in Perth did some investigation and survey trips and designed a service. They advertised for sub-contractors and 150 applied. Agents were appointed in all the destination towns. The launch date for the service by Comet was February 1971, but a cyclone brought rain that blocked the roads, so the inaugural run was 2nd March.

The plan was a 6.30pm departure from Perth on each week day. There were two men in each truck to alternate the driving. After 1225km at Nanutarra Roadhouse they would meet another truck that was based at Nanutarra, which would take the freight for the inland destinations. The Perth truck would continue up the coast road delivering to the towns and mines as far as Port Hedland. All those places would be reached next day, and the agent would deliver around the town. Port Hedland would be reached after business hours that day, but consignees could get a night-time delivery if they wished. That service, 1775km, in about 24 hours, was unprecedented and turned out to be a winner. It was not cheap, but price was secondary when

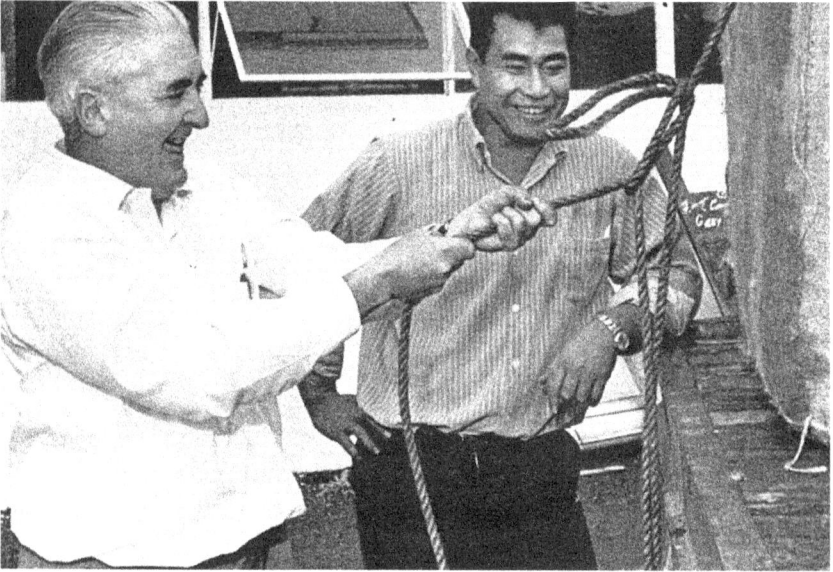

In New Zealand, Ken Thomas joins Maori truck driver, John Meredith, on the job.

much of the freight was equipment and spare parts for the huge mining and infrastructure projects. Holdups were much more expensive to them.

Again TNT led the field. The executives Ken had selected had identified a need, and found the solution. No wonder Ken was proud of them.

Alltrans had brought to the merged businesses their New Zealand experience and organisation. NZ had been discovered by Alltrans in 1964. Like Australia there were restrictions on road transport, and trucks were limited to a 40 mile limit when in competition with rail.

The NZ Railways were very interested to hear of the Australian experience with bulk loading, and were keen to work with Alltrans to provide such a service for NZ. This was arranged and grew quickly: in four years, 17 Alltrans depots were established in NZ.

The initial Auckland building was old and obsolete, and much of the freight handling was in the open, so a new 50,000 sq ft terminal was designed. It was built by TNT on railway land at Remuera, the biggest terminal in the country and a vast improvement on the previous depot.

Ken Thomas flew to Auckland to attend the opening in May 1969 and was interviewed by the press. Ken told them he intended to get a working knowledge of the local transport system the best possible way. He said, "I want to spend a morning with a Maori truck driver on the job—this way I will learn more about the subject than in any boardroom."

The success of the Alltrans/TNT service was highlighted by Mr P. Geddes, the General Manager of the NZ Railways when the TNT terminal was opened at Dunedin in September 1968. Mr Geddes said that there had been a saving in three years of $75 million in railway costs, due to the increase of efficiency, modernisation and the attraction of new business, and bulk loading was an important part of that.

Then there was a move to Canada. In December 1969, TNT made a bid for Gill Interprovincial Lines of Canada. The offer of $5.25 million was acceptable, and Gill's 450 employees became part of the TNT family. Gill had 335 trailers and was the biggest inter-province road carrier in Canada. The company was managed from their headquarters in Vancouver. The Canadian management and staff were left in place, but Peter Abeles made a number of trips to Canada to supervise the integration into TNT. The President of Gill, Mr Harold Freeman, was given a seat on the TNT Board of Directors.

Early in 1970, the takeover of the California-based road transport company, Walk Up Merchants Express, was announced. The name was changed to All-trans Express, and Peter Abeles was to consolidate the US management team, and supervise the company going as fast as possible into the USA market.

While Ken Thomas was interested in these overseas operations he was happy to leave their oversight to Peter Abeles. Ken was more interested in Australia, and the extension and smooth running of his traditional services. In his chairman's address to the annual meeting of the shareholders, on 19th September 1970 Ken said, "There is still a great deal of scope inside Australia for us to develop land transport, especially by more intensive utilisation of our rail forwarding facilities and our TNT trains."

Another development in 1969 was the courier girls service. With the growth of the company, there were now a number of offices and terminals, and this created a big need to get documents and information to and from them. With no computer links and no fax machines, items like freight manifests, figures for the computer inputs, correspondence, reports, and weekly statistics to management had to be sent as hard copies. Until this time it was done in taxis, or taking an employee from their normal job. Other companies had similar needs, and they would pay for a reliable courier service.

It was decided that TNT should establish a properly organised courier service for themselves and other clients. Attractive young women, in a distinctive uniform and eye-catching vehicle, were recruited and trained. The service caught on quickly and in a few months there were six TNT couriers running round Sydney, and the branches in other cities were also introducing them.

Ken Thomas was asked by a journalist from the *Financial Review* about the social responsibilities of big business. Ken told him that it was the same for any business, big or small; and it was "to simply do a first class job. If every business does its own thing and does it well, then it follows that the whole community is efficient and therefore prosperous, and can afford to pay the necessary taxes to support all sorts of modern altruistic welfare projects in the fields of health, education, culture and progress."

There was a great respect for Ken and his achievements and he was becoming increasingly well known. Typical of this was an invitation to address the Institute of Transport on 26th March 1971.

Ken referred to the Bureau of Transport Economics which the Federal Government had created in 1970, as the bureau was then recruiting staff. "What would the bureau do?" Ken asked. "Would it do more than research, would it advise the government to create?"

Naturally Ken had his own ideas on what should be the answer to that question, and he spelt out what he thought should happen. "The drum note should be, rail, rail, rail." The problem, as always, was finance, and in particular, the financial arrangements between the state and federal governments. Ken said that in 1969/70 there was 10 times more federal money spent on roads than on rail. Why? Because, he said, the Commonwealth Bureau of Roads was a strong lobby group but there was not a Commonwealth Bureau of Railways to push for rail money. Nobody was advocating the inherent advantages of rail, and the benefits that could be achieved in price and service.

One of the complications was that freight transport and passenger transport were considered together, when they were completely different, and should be evaluated separately. Passenger transport lost money, but properly organised freight transport was profitable.

Ken gave his audience a laugh, and something to think about when he quoted from a letter, written by the Governor of New York to the US President Andrew Jackson in 1829.

The Governor wrote:

"The canal system of this country is being threatened by the spread of a new form of transportation known as 'railroads'. Serious unemployment will result, captains, cooks, horsemen and lock tenders will be left without work, and farmers unable to sell their hay. Boat builders will suffer. Canal boats are absolutely essential to the defence of the USA. Railroad engines travel at 15 miles per hour, and the Almighty never intended that people should travel at such breakneck speed."

Ken concluded his address with the prediction that the commonwealth would not lead, but just preserve the Menzies doctrine that *"the function of government was to administer, not to create."*

Ken's role as the father figure leading and enjoying the contact with his staff is highlighted in his 1971 Christmas message. He wrote: *"In the past few weeks I have had the very great pleasure of attending Christmas parties in Brisbane, Perth, Adelaide and Melbourne. They were terrific. The capacity of our young people to have a whale of a time at a well behaved swinging night out is a joy to see. It is obvious that there is a great deal of solid friendship and mutual respect, and I think this is especially strong at TNT."*

He concluded: *"In the transport game there is no standing still. The ability of our management to conceive and venture with new ideas, and of the staff to execute them is our real strength."*

In the 1972 New Year's honours list was the knighthood of Peter Abeles. Subsequently he was known as Sir Peter Abeles. The knighthood was conferred by the Queen for Peter's 'Service to Business and the Arts'.

There was speculation about why Peter Abeles was knighted, and Ken Thomas was not. Ken was not afraid to let it be known that he did not believe in honours. When a journalist asked Ken about this Ken told him: "Probably because the government know I would never accept one of their honours—which I regard as totally invidious—and they don't want to risk the embarrassment of my refusal."

In 1977, there was a Silver Jubilee Medal struck, as it was the Silver Jubilee of the Queen, to mark her 25 years on the throne. Ken received a medal in the mail, with no explanation of why it was awarded to him. Ken felt he had done nothing extraordinary to deserve it, so he sent it back, politely declining to accept it. So if Ken had been considered for a knighthood or another honour that view would have prevailed.

Peter Abeles, however, was a man who sought connections with other powerful men. There was a close friendship between Peter and Rob Askin, Premier of NSW from 1965 to 1975. Peter and Rob met frequently for poker games, and it was suspected that this close association was instrumental in Askin adding Abeles name to the list of nominees for a knighthood.

In June 1972, Ross Cribb was awarded an OBE, an Officer of the British Empire. Ken told the staff in 'Freight Notes' how he had befriended Ross back in 1954, and recruited him as a management trainee. Naturally Ken was delighted that his protégé had done so well.

Ken's passion for road safety meant he was very pleased to announce the results of the first year of the Sights On Safety (SOS) scheme. TNT's interstate road drivers were able to win merchandise from a contest that awarded points for accident free driving. To gain a perfect score a driver had to have a 12 month period without a scratch on his vehicle. The result was a reduction of 28% in minor accidents, and a healthy 73% reduction in major accidents.

For the TNT board one of the big issues at that time was Ansett Transport Industries Ltd. This company had been started by Reg Ansett back in 1935, and initially was a small and struggling airline. After the war, Labor Prime Minister Chifley had wanted to nationalise the airline industry, but this was disallowed by the High Court. To have some part in the industry, the Federal government started Trans Australia Airlines (TAA). In 1957 Ansett bought ANA, a larger airline which had been established by the Tasmanian Holyman family in the 1930s, now to become Ansett-ANA.

The Federal Government had a two airline policy, so the only competitor for Ansett-ANA was the government-owned TAA. Fare prices were the same and flight schedules were very similar. No cheap air fares in those days. The Government controlled the industry with regulations restricting the import of aircraft.

Reg Ansett had started the business in Hamilton Victoria, and it was now based in Melbourne, so it was always a very Victorian-centred organisation, and listed on the Melbourne Stock Exchange.

Ken Thomas saw Ansett as a means for TNT to be more involved with air transport, and to integrate with the other services they offered. They were offering freight transport by road, rail and sea and their next objective was air freight. W.R.Carpenter and Boral each had a parcel of Ansett shares for sale, so TNT bought them all, and gained 23.5% of the Ansett shares.

"VICTORIAN RULES!" — This is how Steve, the Sydney Sunday Mirror's cartoonist, saw Sir Henry Bolte's role in the Ansett takeover bid.

'MAY DAY, MAY DAY, COME IN GOVERNMENT,,,,GOVERNMENT,,,,'

Top: Bolte, as referee, interferes in the Thomas chase of Ansett.

Bottom: Ken has 23% of Ansett, but wants the rest!

TNT then expected to be invited to nominate a director to join the Ansett board, which was the normal course of events. This would be the way to integrate both companies' operations for the benefit of the public. But instead of an invitation, TNT received abuse from Ansett, so TNT made a formal offer to take over all of Ansett.

When that was known to the Victorian Premier Sir Henry Bolte, legislation was introduced and passed by the Victorian Parliament that specifically prohibited TNT from buying more Ansett shares. TNT had to stop buying these shares, but wanted to contest the matter.

This was seen as a state interests' battle, with TNT in the NSW corner, fighting Ansett from Victoria. Bolte had used the need to maintain Ansett as an Australian company and not owned or controlled from overseas as a reason for his action.

On 27th April 1972, the day the Victorian Parliament agreed to this restriction, TNT withdrew their takeover offer.

That evening Ken Thomas was interviewed by Richard Carlton on the ABC TV program, This Day Tonight, which was shown Australia wide. Ken said he saw the offer as a simple business proposition that would be for the good of both companies, good for the staff, good for the shareholders and for the good of Australia.

Ken said, "It is a matter of fulfilling a function—the function is to produce the best transport system in Australia. TNT's motto has always been; 'Not the biggest, but the best.'" Ken had explained that about 98% of the TNT shares were now owned by Australians. The TNT shares that had been acquired by the Transport Development Group of the U.K. had been sold to Australians.

In the interview, Ken said that he personally could not co-operate with Sir Reginald Ansett because he thought that, in going to the government for protection, Sir Reg had not acted in the best interests of the Ansett shareholders. He had exerted tremendous influence and pressure on the Victorian Government and on some federal politicians, which had resulted in the setting up a Senate enquiry in Canberra. What had particularly got up Ken's nose was a demand by Reg Ansett for TNT to reduce the 23% shareholding down to 10%. "Colossal impudence of the man, telling TNT what to do; I resent it," thundered Ken to hundreds of thousands of TV viewers.

There was a loud roar of approval from many of these people. Ken was swamped with telegrams and letters from all over Australia, applauding him for expressing his views, and standing up to Ansett and Bolte.

The idea of being involved with Ansett as part of the whole transport service did not fade; it was discussed by the TNT board. The tension with Sir Reg Ansett cooled off, and there were talks to find a compromise.

In June an agreement was reached, and on 28th June 1972 the press carried an announcement that TNT and Ansett had 'buried the hatchet'. TNT were able to keep the shares they had, which was 23% of Ansett capital. However, TNT's voting rights were restricted to 10%. TNT would be able to appoint one director to the Ansett board, and Peter Abeles was to be that director. Sir Peter told the press that this arrangement suited TNT, and would allow them to work with Ansett.

In another controversial interview on radio, Ken was asked about a policy he had followed for years about not employing university graduates. While Ken had two degrees, he kept quiet about that and did not let others know.

Asked why he felt this way Ken said, "Had I applied for a position it would have damaged my chance of getting a job...because of the suspicion that I regarded myself as better than those I was to work with." Ken went on to say that there is nothing complicated about transport, so it did not need a university degree. He said that the best way to train a manager was on the job experience. Ken said, "There are more and more businesses, big businesses that have crashed, and one of the features of these businesses that crash is they have academics at the top."

Ken's policy of not employing university graduates was well known, and is interesting as it conflicted with his own success, carrying his two degrees. However it does highlight the lack of courses offered by the universities relevant to business in general, and transport in particular. In those days a choice between an accountancy or economics degree was about the limit.

In 1954 the first tertiary transport course in New South Wales was offered by the Sydney Technical College, with a four year Certificate Course in Transport Administration. This was sponsored by the Institute of Transport, and courses were offered about the same time in the other states too.

The 1972 annual report to shareholders told them about TNT Plaza, a twin tower complex in Lawson Square, Redfern. A 19,000 square feet block of land had been acquired, previously the site of an hotel and theatre. The two towers of 12 stories would be identical. One block would become the computer division, and the company's head office. The other tower would contain a tavern and there would be some office space for tenants. They would be connected by a public arcade, and landscaped gardens. A garage for 150 cars would be adjacent, with underground secure space for the armoured car division. Design of the building had started in 1972, and construction was completed in 1976. TNT occupied about two-thirds of the space and the balance was rented to tenants.

The buildings, right beside Redfern railway station, did a lot to boost TNT's profile because on the roof of each building was a large TNT neon sign. The complex could be seen for many kilometres in each direction, and hundreds of thousands of train passengers traveling to and from the city each day could not miss it.

Before moving to the twin towers, Ken Thomas and Peter Abeles operated from head office in Macquarie Street, near the Opera House overlooking Circular Quay. They later observed that while they enjoyed the view there, it was not the same as being close to Mascot, Alexandria, Cooks River and the industrial belt where the work was done, and the business grew. They enjoyed that view much more.

The annual report told the shareholders the results for the year to 30th June 1972.

"YOU SHOWED THE WAY, AND OTHERS FOLLOWED IN MANY INNOVATIONS IN TRANSPORT, IN AUSTRALIA."

—*RALPH DAVIS, MAYNE NICKLESS MANAGING DIRECTOR*

CHAPTER 14

THE DISMISSAL

Thursday 13th of July 1972 was to turn out to be a significant day in Ken Thomas's life.

On that day he gave the second Genesis Lecture to a Sydney University Students Group. The topic was, 'The Role of the University in Social Change'.

Ken said, "These days free speech is left to the working class, farmers, small businessmen, to the universities and the media. The universities are most likely to give the lead in a philosophy for living. That is the big need...the practical action comes from people who have pre-thought their basics, and do not fiddle around as social exigencies arise...

"We are on the verge of a breakthrough that will be positive, rather than merely destructive, but in creating there will be an inevitable destruction... The destruction will be in two areas riddled with superstition. The first is religion, the second psychology.

"The main superstition is religion, with its feeble mindedness about mortality, the supernatural, the soul and the precious ego. The second superstition is psychology, which is all about the psyche which assumes that the psyche is a miraculous inner man, independent of and overriding the body. Thought is merely a product of the brain. What is needed is a positive programme that reduces religion to legend, and psychology to physiology.

The two main elements of a philosophy for social change are:

That the greatest good is happiness.

That we are all accidents of birth and circumstances (mainly genetic accidents). Our conceited and precious egos are silly and misery making.

The right place for such a philosophy to germinate is Australia, because Australians are realist, light-hearted and humble.

Do not conclude that I want to discard the Christian ethic; it is a philosophy of happiness and love, its best elements will survive. 'Be of Good cheer' was a phrase constantly used by Jesus. The Presbyterian shorter catechism's first question is answered, 'Man's chief end is to glorify God, and enjoy Him for ever'. Substitute nature for God, and I am completely on side.

The American Constitution, copied by the Vietnam Constitution says 'Man has an inalienable right to life, liberty and the pursuit of happiness'.

We are social beings and enjoy life in the company of others, and we need to live with happy people. One feature of a happy society is a society free of ignorance, fear and superstition, especially religious superstition. Each of us is not the master of his fate; it is a natural product of birth and circumstances."

The next day, the Sydney *Daily Telegraph* had a story with a huge headline:

TNT HEAD SAYS DESTROY RELIGION.

The text went on to quote Ken as saying superstition of religion was a terrible impediment to progress.

The afternoon paper, *The Sun,* had an editorial:

OUR OWN DOUBTING THOMAS

TNT the transport giant has taken on some pretty tough customers in its path to the top. Now TNT's boss has over stretched even his own considerable power. He has taken on God.

The paper had a story, and quotes from a Roman Catholic spokesman, who said, *"Mr Thomas has to be either joking or serious. If he is joking it is in bad taste. If he is serious he lacks an awareness of religion's great contribution to progress."*

Rev Alan Walker was the Acting President of the Methodist Church in NSW; he knew Ken personally, as Ken had supported The Central Methodist Mission, so said, *"Mr Thomas knows a great deal about earthly transport, but I am not sure he knows so much about heavenly truth.*

"I am sure he has a much higher regard for the Christian faith than his remarks would indicate. His fine humanitarianism comes from his Christian background and I suspect he knows that."

Those explosive headlines caused quite a stir.

CHAPTER 14

TNT HEAD SAYS DESTROY RELIGION

Superstition of religion was a terrible impediment to progress, the chairman of Thomas Nationwide Transport (Mr K. W. Thomas) said yesterday.

Religion, with all its feeblemindedness about immortality, the soul, supernatural things and about the ~~precious ego~~," needed to be destroyed, he said.

Mr Thomas was speaking at the second lecture in the 1972 Genesis Lecture Series at Sydney University.

Speaking on the "Role of the University in Social Change," he said leadership in thought and philosophy was the main role of universities.

There was a great need in society for a breakthrough in these, he said.

It needed to be positive and constructive but in the process of creation "we must destroy".

He said there were two superstitions which need to be destroyed.

"One is the superstition of religion."

The other was psychology and "all this business about the psyche".

Addicted

The Minister for Customs (Mr Chipp) had been quoted as saying drug addicts claimed smoking marihuana led to a "psychological dependency just as compulsive as physical addiction".

"To my mind a drug addict is just physically addicted," Mr Thomas said.

Two of the adverse effects of belief in religious superstition were the present trouble in Ireland and the Vietnam war, he said.

The Vietnam war had been "primarily due" to certain American leaders, particularly one man who believed it was his God-given mission, to hold back Communism and stop atheism.

Mr Thomas said, however, he was not against Christian philosophy.

Daily Telegraph. 14th of July, 1972.

220

Our own doubting Thomas...

TNT, the transport giant, has taken on some pretty tough customers in its path to the top.

Now TNT's boss, Mr Thomas, has over-stretched even his own considerable power.

He's taken on God.

EDITORIAL

The business king opened his mind on this delicate subject in an extraordinary lecture to Sydney University students yesterday.

Superstition of religion was a terrible impediment to progress, he said.

Religion with all its feebleness about immortality, the soul and supernatural things needed to be destroyed.

He plunged on in these deep and dangerous waters. He blamed religion for Ireland and Vietnam.

Mr Thomas is tragically, grievously wrong.

Politics and history are the curse of Vietnam and Ireland. Religion is the easiest to blame.

But religion has been the great and only comfort in the lives of countless millions for centuries.

It has provided — and still provides — a depth of value in all our lives.

It inspires trust and faith. It nurtures love and understanding.

In today's world, greedy for change and progress — whatever that is — the shining stars are success and commercialism.

But people who have nothing will always have something precious if they have a love of God and live by it.

The Sun. 14th of July, 1972.

221

Ross Cribb reported that on the day of the *Telegraph* story, a Friday, he had taken 50 phone calls from customers and staff. Ross said the least Ken could do was to lay off religion, and that he (Ross) was making a complaint. But to whom would that be addressed, as Peter Abeles, the managing director was overseas.

Over the weekend Peter was informed of Ken's speech and that some of the other directors thought it was time for Ken to go. Peter did not disagree.

On Monday morning, in Peter Abeles's office, Fred Millar and two other directors, Sir Ian Potter and John Horrocks, met Ken and asked him to resign. There were ten directors on the board, the others being Peter Abeles, Ross Cribb, Harold Freeman, Bill Martin, George Rockey and Ken Smith. There was no agreement that the matter was important enough to be left until the full board should be called together. Fred Millar said the board would make the most generous settlement possible, which would be discussed when Peter returned. Ken replied that if the board wanted him to resign he would do so, but that did not mean that he felt he should resign. When Ken wrote his resignation letter, he said it would take effect as soon as convenient. Fred Millar asked Ken to change that to 'resign forthwith', which he did. The three board members accepted the resignation that day.

Ken was very upset. He knew that Fred Millar was out to get the chairman's job, and he was extremely disappointed that Peter Abeles and Ross Cribb had deserted him and allowed that to happen. Although he tried to put on a brave face, Ken carried that bitterness for the rest of his life.

There was then an exchange of cables (an overseas telegram) between Ken and Peter Abeles, who was still in Canada.

Peter said to Ken:

Dear Ken very sad and distressed news sorry was absent stop your friendship and cooperation gave me best working years of my life stop hope you will find great happiness and joy regards in old friendship see you after return. Peter.

Ken cabled back:

Your very nice cable received but it is still a fact that you were consulted before my dismissal and approved it stop advisable everyone's interests straighten my position before public appearance at contact club next Thursday stop regardless of anything now said history will record that tnt thommoed as with a tomahawk its founder chairman stop it would have been much more intelligent to kick me upstairs as a consultant and it may still not be too late but will be after next Thursday noon Sydney time stop are you aware that financial review carried a leading article last Wednesday under bold heading letting businessmen speak out suggest it would be unrealistic to imagine thing has blown over unless overt and practical action is taken immediately stop regards Thomas.

A week later Ken was in Cairns and he had had time to reflect on the situation. He wrote to Peter:

Dear Peter

As arranged by yourself and the board members, I was dismissed last Monday. The only reason given by Fred or by anyone else was the fact of the expression of my private views (having nothing to do with business), which are not acceptable. Not acceptable to whom? In reality the whole affair was mediaeval, saved by exposure by my good humour.

Evidence of a plot to oust Ken was revealed in the next paragraph of Ken's letter:

*"In view of the circumstances I presume that the most generous possible settle-
ment alluded to by Fred would considerably exceed the $200,000 figure men-
tioned by yourself some months ago when you raised the matter of my possible
retirement in the remote future."*

For some weeks the papers had stories about Ken's resignation and what had
brought it about. Ken kept a straight face and said it was company policy to
retire at 60, and he was only a year away from that. He declined a couple of
appearances on TV, including the ABC's *This Day Tonight*, as he thought that
a TV interview might flush out the truth.

It does seem incredible that the founder of the company, and chairman of the
board was ambushed in this way. There is no indication that Ken's activity
and campaigning against the Vietnam War, five and six years earlier, had disturbed the other directors, the employees, the shareholders or the customers.
The report of 50 people making a phone call based on a newspaper account
of the speech is a very flimsy reason to sack a man who had done so much,
for so many, for so long.

Joy Annard was Peter Abeles's secretary for 40 years from 1954, but she was in
hospital on that memorable day, and so not a witness to the encounter in Sir
Peter's office. However Joy is mystified as to why Ken did not fight back. "The
press loved him," she said. "Ken should have made a statement to clarify his
position and it would have been printed."

As it turned out, Fred Millar was the policeman, judge, executioner and
beneficiary, all done in a matter of a few hours. Justice was not done. Had
the three directors decided to propose a special meeting a few weeks later

when the issue had cooled down, and with all directors present, a calm and reasoned arrangement could no doubt have been made for Ken to wind down and retire with dignity.

FRED MILLAR

Fred was interviewed in March 2013 and asked about his role in the dismissal. He readily acknowledged that he did "tap Ken on the shoulder" after the meeting with two other directors. Fred said that they felt they had the authority, and it did not need a meeting of the whole board.

Fred gave as their reasons the university speech, and another reason was that Ken had exceeded his authority in the TV interview on the Ansett takeover attempt. Fred says that after the Senate enquiry on the proposal he (Fred) was to be the sole spokesman for TNT on the matter. That meant the chairman (Ken) and managing director (Peter Abeles) were supposed to remain silent.

Fred was elected to be chairman of the board to succeed Ken and remained in the chair until 1997. Despite the long term on the board, Fred admitted he knew little about the operations and had no idea of Ken's achievements in the development of Australian transport.

Letters flowed to Ken from all over Australia. Some were from former and current employees, thanking him for their careers. Others were from strangers who had been impressed with what he had achieved for the development of Australian transport. Ken felt the need to meet many of his friends for a farewell so decided to make visits, and throw a party for them. Ken told the board he would do this at his own expense, and the parties with employees would not be in working hours.

Harold Freeman, a director of TNT living in Vancouver Canada, wrote a letter of regret about Ken's resignation. Although a director, he had not been consulted and said that Ken was too young to retire for the reasons stated.

Harold wrote, *"Your talents as a chairman will be difficult to replace. In my long experience in the corporate world in this country, I would find it difficult to designate anyone who could match you. I am genuinely sorry to see you withdraw."*

Another moving tribute came from Ralph Davis, the Managing Director of Mayne Nickless Ltd, who was in London when he heard the news. Ralph had been in transport for many years and was widely respected. During Ralph's term at the helm, TNT had overtaken Mayne Nickless to become the biggest transport company in Australia; a lesser man than Ralph would have been sour about that.

Ralph wrote, *"News reached me at a distance of 12,000 miles of your retirement as Chairman of TNT Ltd. I could not let this opportunity pass without a brief note acknowledging the very great success that has attended your activities in transport. I realise that in recent days active management was in the hands of others but Ken, I want to say to you, with respect to all others, that you showed the way and others followed in many innovations in transport in Australia.*

"In the course of it you often sacrificed personal feelings for the integrity of your enterprise and this paid off. Even some of the people who have been through your hands and are now in other companies still hold you in very high regard. You taught us all a lot. I look forward to having a chat with you again one of these days."

This handsome tribute from Ralph Davis is even more enhanced by the fact that Ralph was a strong Christian, as leading member of the Methodist Church in Melbourne. Ralph in his concluding paragraph said, *"I am going to take issue with you on your comments on religion, but that will wait for another day."*

Another letter came from Max Luff of Albury Border Transport Pty Ltd:

."..I particularly enjoyed your recent joust with Sir Reginald Ansett. On the surface it appears that your departure was sparked by your ability to say exactly what you think about whatever. Let us hope that people's obsession with conformity has not forced you from the industry.

The purpose of this note is to say thank you for your contribution to the industry in which I am very actively engaged...It is sad that you have left the industry when you still have an enormous amount to contribute."

Ken took up with the board the matter of his retirement terms. The figure of $300,000 was suggested but it had to be approved by the shareholders at their annual meeting on 30th October 1972. They did agree to that payment.

There was also to be an annual retainer as a consultant of $35,000 for five years. This was later extended and it continued until at least 1990.

Forty years later, looking back at Ken's dismissal, and trying to make sense of it, some aspects become possible.

Rhody Thomas, Ken's eldest son, says that his father was tired of the 'establishment' that Peter Abeles had gradually brought to the board. Ken thought Fred Millar was a "corporate crook," and the lawyers and accountants who knew nothing about transport had gained control of the company. Rhody says his father was no longer enjoying board meetings. Ken had dabbled in other business arrangements, none of which went well, so the idea of a lump sum payout had a lot of appeal to Ken.

Ken may also have wanted to make a quick exit to protect the share price. No doubt had there been a brawl in the boardroom, the shareholders would have become very jittery and decided to get out. That would have decreased the value of the Thomas family share holdings.

Then Ken could be understood if he felt that he had done his job. He had taken a business he started with one truck up to the largest transport company in Australia. TNT was larger than Mayne Nickless, with their 60 year start. Ken showed little interest in the overseas operations, they were all a plaything for Peter Abeles, and expansion overseas was where the future growth would be.

Despite the turmoil over his dismissal Ken kept the appointment to address the Sydney Contact Group at a lunch on 27th July. However, he spoke on the 'Social Responsibility of Businessmen'.

Ken said that a businessman had the same responsibility as everyone else, 80% of that was to simply pull your weight. There was no duty we so much underrate as the duty to be happy, and one way to happiness is to do a good job.

Ken went on to tell the audience of the transport industry's record of improving services, but at the same time dramatically lowering the prices for the movement of freight.

To amplify his point, some figures were quoted. In 1946, when he started in the transport business, the ruling rate from Sydney to Melbourne was $16 per ton, now it was $15. To take the inflation that had occurred into account, money had depreciated by a factor of 21 in that time. That meant road transport rates had fallen from about $50 to $15 in the last 26 years: "An amazing achievement" Ken said.

"It came about because of a tremendous growth in rail transport," Ken continued. "More particularly in organisational methods that have been developed for integrating forwarding agents in the local road business with rail transport. The transport industry offered to pay the railways $6000 per month, to haul a rail wagon between Sydney and Melbourne. That wagon does three return trips to and from Melbourne each week. The railways are paid monthly in advance, whether or not there is a load for it. It is superb business from the railway point of view. The marginal cost for them to run an extra train is very small. Their costs are in building and maintaining the infrastructure, the tracks, the signalling system, and all the overheads of running the railways."

There were some figures too. Ken said that the amount of rail freight handled by the forwarder companies between Sydney, Melbourne and Brisbane had risen from 7000 tons in 1950, to 70,000 tons in 1960 to 700,000 tons in 1970. With pride he told about TNT then having a full train-load of freight each night each way between Sydney and Melbourne, bringing a decrease of trucks on the road and the saving of lives that had resulted. Ken's modesty did not allow him to say that his own efforts were largely responsible for such an achievement.

Ken told the audience that more government money should be spent on railways, and that too much was going to roads. He criticised the Liberal Party who had been in government in Canberra for the previous 22 years, and said a Labor Government would have done more rail improvements.

Then Ken, always the visionary, thought of the future with some crystal ball gazing objectives for transport.

In the year 2000 we could see ships, either private or commonwealth owned, 100,000-ton Lash Type Nozzle propelled nuclear powered jet ship, with a speed of 35 knots, and a crew of 10, for the coastal trade, linking the cities where most Australians live.

By rail, interstate hover trains travelling at 200mph could compete with the nuclear powered ships.

For the air: Abandon the two airline policy, maintain safety standards, and after most of the newcomers go broke, permit the leading operator to have a fleet of dirigibles on interstate routes.

Road: Whatever else happens, retain the Australian principle, unique in the world, of the right to unrestricted entry into the road transport industry.

In the 21st century it is interesting to look back at these dreams. The only one that comes close to Ken's fantasy is the road transport, as that was easy... to do nothing.

Ken could not hide his unhappiness over the dismissal. Evidence of this was his withdrawal from a commitment to visit Harden, his birthplace.

In May 1972 Ken was advised that there was to be a 'Back to Harden-Murrumburrah' week, and that as a distinguished ex-resident of the district he was invited to open the ball on 29th September. Ken had quickly and enthusiastically accepted the invitation, and said that he and his wife Anne would stay six days as he had rarely visited his home town since leaving as a boy.

After his dismissal, Ken wrote again to the Shire Clerk of Demondrille Council, who was chairman of the organising committee. Ken said: *"Some publicity has occurred concerning my private beliefs, particularly that I am an atheist and that I believe religion has a damaging influence in society.*

This complicates the position. I think it would be advisable to withdraw my acceptance, in the interests of your having an harmonious and happy celebration."

The Shire Clerk, Mr. A.J. Wickham responded expressing his disappointment, and saying that he was not aware of the publicity Ken had referred to.

Peter Abeles said in the next issue of the staff magazine:

"Every nation, every family, and every company is richer if it has a tradition. Our tradition comes from our founder, Mr K. W. Thomas.

As you all know by now, Mr Thomas after a quarter of a century has resigned his position as chairman of the TNT group. His ability and knowhow as a transport man, is now part of Australia's history.

However, on behalf of the staff and myself, I would like to say good bye to Ken Thomas the man."

It has been my privilege to work with Mr Thomas very closely during the past five years. I have always found him to be a most understanding and good human being, and I am sure we all wish him a very rewarding and successful retirement, which he so richly deserves.

We would like to assure him that his name will live for all times in the hearts of the people who worked with him, and in his company's history.

I appeal to Mr Thomas to make part of his time available, to act as an adviser to myself and the board. His help would be invaluable, and it would give us an opportunity to keep in close contact with him."

True to his word, Ken kept his promise to do some farewell trips at his own expense to many of the branches.

In Perth they brought the Christmas party forward to 17th October to make it a big occasion for Ken. Arthur Bray was in charge and made it a memorable night, a roaring success. The report said, "The staff in WA paid tribute to Ken and are all sorry to see him retire." A special present for him was arranged: a leading Perth cartoonist was commissioned to produce an excellent coloured cartoon, depicting humorous aspects of retirement.

So Ken went from TNT with the memory of some great years, some tremendous achievements and a host of friends who really regretted his departure. Letters poured in for a long while, from staff, business contacts and some people who had never met him, but knew of his achievements, all thanking him and wishing him well.

However, Ken was still in the public eye. The media were still trying to get more information from Ken.

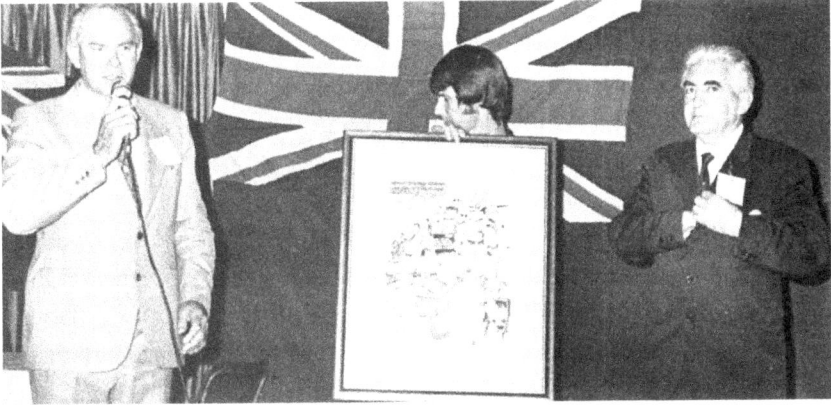

Top: In Perth, Arthur Bray makes a farewell presentation to Ken.

Bottom: On the floor pouring a beer for Bill Weekes at the Brisbane farewell.

In November 1972, Ken was invited by the ABC to be interviewed on the *Four Corners* TV programme with Gordon Barton. The theme was the choices people make about participating in, or dropping out of society. In particular the interviewer wanted to explore the proposition that busy businessman were not really happy.

Ken said that it was the regimentation and anonymity of a large business, such as TNT had become, that was the problem. For this reason he was glad of his release from the TNT board. Ken slammed the structures: "There is pressure, appointments, luncheons, having to always say the right thing, so having to think twice before saying anything. Criticism of the government cannot be done, because it is necessary to stay on side with the government. People in that situation dare not come out and say what they think; they have so many obligations and complications. They cannot be happy, because they are not free."

Gordon Barton told the viewers that happiness came from the sense of doing something that is reasonably worthwhile, and taxing your abilities. "If an active person stops being active, very frequently it destroys him, a very sad thing. It is a form of death. If these people go off and go fishing, I believe it is a waste," he concluded.

CHAPTER 15

THE TRANSPORT VISIONARY

The success that Ken Thomas had had with the development of rail transport gave him the inspiration and determination to continue that crusade, and tell others. After his dismissal Ken made himself known as a transport consultant and kept up his high profile with many speeches.

While still chairman of TNT, on 9th July 1971, Ken addressed the Western Australia Chartered Institute of Transport Seminar in Perth, on the subject, 'Growth of Long Distance Rail Freight'. First he gave a blast to the Bureau of Transport Economics who had been very slow in producing figures on the transport of freight across Australia.

The latest figures then available were from 1962-63. The statistics showed that ton miles share of the task was; Sea 50%; Rail 23%; Road 27%; Air 0.1%.

Ken said his estimate was that rail had gone up to 30% in the eight years since then, and road had lost that 7%.

From his contacts in the New South Wales Railways he knew that interstate tons carried by rail had increased by 57% in 1970 over the tonnage of 1964. Standardising the rail gauge was an important factor.

However, Ken gave credit also to the Hughes and Vale decision which had meant *"rail had emerged from its slumber."* Rail now had to compete. The railways had made vast improvements in rolling stock and track, they had reduced overheads, and decreased freight rates by over 30%. As a result rail volumes went up, and they were making money on freight haulage. Ken's figure was a profit of $22m on freight. What held the public attention was the overall loss by New South Wales rail, because the passenger services had lost $46m.

Ken said this profitability on freight had been unique to Australia. New Zealand and Canada had now followed suit, by adopting the successful Australian methods. His natural modesty would not allow him to say that it was TNT that had led the transport industry in this area, because of the genius of Ken Thomas himself.

Ken's theme, repeated at every opportunity, was that government spending should be more on rail, and less on the roads.

As he was addressing a West Australia group, a long way from the eastern states, Ken shared with the seminar his vision of a coastal shipping line and the nuclear powered jet ship that could do 35 knots. He also suggested one maritime union to overcome all the demarcation disputes.

Ken was on a campaign and was invited by many organisations to speak, and to use his experience and imagination in raising the profile of transport in Australia. He continued to champion rail as the best way to move most freight, and decried the way the Australian governments were not responding with spending money on rail improvements, particularly on track works.

Ken floated his 'Southern Cross Plan'. There was a line running east-west across the continent, from Sydney through Orange to Broken Hill, and then on to South Australia and Perth.

There was also a north-south line from Victoria through Albury to Harden, and the branch line to the main western line at Blayney, through Orange, and on to Dubbo, then a line to Werris Creek to meet the northern tablelands line to Wallangarra, on the Queensland border. Ken advocated that there should be a major rail junction at Orange which would be the centre of the cross. From there freight could flow to all mainland capitals.

The work already done with rail gauge standardisation meant the only gauge change needed would be the 240km from Wallangarra to Brisbane. However, there would be work needed to upgrade the track, particularly the western areas in New South Wales. At every opportunity Ken spoke about this and did his best to arouse public interest and support.

The barrier he faced is still in place in the 21st century, as Australia's rail infrastructure has not kept up with the demands. Politicians are always more concentrated on spending money on vote winning projects. Voters are not turned on about the location of rail tracks for goods trains.

FORTY TWO YEARS LATER

The Southern Cross Plan was the purpose of a Melbourne to Brisbane Rail Symposium at Parkes in June 2012. It was not quite the same as Ken's dream. The centre of the cross would be at Parkes, not Orange, and then via Narromine, Narrabri, Moree and Toowoomba to Brisbane.

The Australian Rail Track Corporation (ARTC) released a report in 2010, which identified this route. It is shorter and seven hours faster than the existing route through Sydney. The estimated cost is $4 billion. The symposium heard that there is currently almost two million tons of cargo each year, originating from and destined for other places that are carried by rail and road through Sydney.

The Sydney congestion makes it necessary to have a four hour ban each weekday for freight trains to use the lines in Sydney that are also used for passenger trains. This limitation on the number of trains increases the use of road transport. Thousands of trucks now regularly use the Newell Highway to bypass Sydney, and trains should be able to do the same.

Parkes has already been seen as a strategic inland centre by rail operator Asciano, trading as Pacific National, with a recent purchase of land there. From Parkes, trains can double stack containers all the way to Perth or Darwin. In 2012, Pacific National have 600 locos and about 13,000 rail wagons, carrying general freight, grain and coal.

The private government partnership intiated by Ken Thomas 60 years earlier has gone a long way.

Not all of Ken's speaking engagements were about transport. In September 1974 he spoke to the Australian Management Society, and gave them his views on management.

There are three qualities, Ken said: "Brains, Work and Health."

"With Brains, be smart enough to be moderate, know your limitations, realise that to be a happy man is more sensible than being a business magnate. Brilliant professional brains are usually poor business men.

The second requirement is Work. The successful man is dedicated, scorns delights, and lives laborious days, acquisitive and slogging. If he has enough brains he will relinquish this one track course in time to enjoy life.

Then Health: "If your body is not fit then your brain is not fit."

Ken also decried to them the power of the union movement and the monopoly they had for certain jobs. He told of expensive demarcation disputes and the owner not being able to handle his own goods, because a union claimed that "right."

Ken said, "The single most important reason of TNT's success was the reporting system, and the weekly profit estimate from every profit centre in Australia. The weekly estimate comes very close to be the actual when the monthly and quarterly figures are added up."

At this time it was two years since Ken had been dismissed by the board of TNT, so he had something to say about its share price. The 50 cent share of 1961 had grown to a value of $2.80 in 1973, and was in 1974 down to 70 cents. Ken wondered why. "Does this prove that expanding through a high share premium was wrong? It may have been better to have concentrated on being the best carriers in Australia, and retaining more profits in the business, instead of upping the dividend; keeping borrowings low, and leaving the share price to look after itself."

Ken was asked to give a lecture at the Joint Services Staff College in Canberra in August 1974. The subject was Australian National Development—Transport.

This invitation had Ken in a bit of a bind, because he wanted to help and give the young people the benefit of his experience, but he found the academic atmosphere of the college hard to take. The staff there acted as superiors and talked theories which conflicted with his own practical and down to earth experiences.

The problem was overcome with Ken agreeing to write a paper, and saying that they should find somebody better qualified to deliver it. An ex-RAAF officer, then a public servant in the Department of Transport in Canberra was then asked to read Ken's paper.

Ken's talks on transport all over Australia were always bought into the political scene, with state governments being responsible for transport, yet all pushing their own barrow and seldom consulting with each other. Ken was pushing for a national approach.

Ken still carried a map showing that 95% of Australians lived in 18% of the land mass, and the other 5% were scattered over 82% of the country. Transport planning should recognise this fact, and act accordingly, not according to state boundaries.

"The six sovereign states are an unfortunate accident of birth, and an obstruction to all good government, especially transport government," he said.

A continual theme was that too much money was being spent on roads and not enough on railways.

A visionary talk was another address to the Western Australian section of the Institute of Transport, this time in 1979.

"If planning a factory, mine or nation, it is not a bad idea to envisage the result, and work steadily towards that," Ken told them.

This is the 'Light on the Hill,' which Ben Chifley is remembered for espousing.

"The ideal transport system is not a system, it is a dynamic river where everything flows, always there, but varying with the change in natural conditions."

Ken argued strongly against a contemporary who had suggested that the Australian Government needs to be not only interested but also involved in the total planning and regulatory aspects of land transport. Ken said such a system would be the worst possible.

'The glory of road transport in Australia is unrestricted entry. Many successful companies would never have started if they had to 'prove the need'. They never had credentials, they just had a go."

But Ken's strongest criticism was for sea transport, and the way the power of the unions was hampering shipping. Stevedoring costs were twice those in European ports. The railways could move a container from Sydney to Melbourne at half the cost of doing that by sea. No wonder Australian interstate general cargo services by sea had died.

Then Ken told a story that would be funny, if it were not true and so serious.

The Federal Government had released the Nimmo report in March 1976, which had looked at the cost and efficiency of freight services between Tasmania and the mainland.

The two existing services were found to be slow and unreliable, and subject to frequent industrial disputes. The report suggested a vessel that could do the return trip in 24 hours, and with some new manning and stevedoring practices.

Gordon Barton, the long-time mate of Ken's, and the founder of IPEC, had seen the opportunities of such a service and asked Ken to help with the establishment of the Tigerline.

A naval architect was commissioned to design a suitable vessel and a feasibility study was done, which proved positive. However for the freight rates to be attractive, control of crew wages was vital.

The concept was to run an 'Aircraft on Waves' container ship, carrying 74 containers between Westernport in southern Victoria, and Devonport in the north of Tasmania. There was to be a daily return service at a speed of 22 knots. Journey time would be nine hours, so no accommodation would be needed. There would be no duties for ordinary seamen; three officers could do it all comfortably.

Such an arrangement was contrary to the industry norm, which was for the crew to include a cook and multiple deckhands, all to do just an hour or so of work. Normally seamen worked four hour shifts, so two crews would be on board.

At first the Seamens Union would not even discuss the matter, then when they did demanded that there be six seamen as well as the three officers. Endless discussions followed, and much speculation about what the seamen would have to do. For every contingency, fires, accidents etc. there was a push button mechanism, and six seamen were not required for that. The union wanted a cook, to prepare lunch for the three officers, but Gordon Barton said there would be a microwave oven, so the food provided could be heated. The union talked about the necessity of a crew man should they have to anchor while on a voyage, and then the rope rewound after the anchor was raised. Gordon Barton said they would cut the rope and leave the anchor, and replace it with a new anchor. Doing that, even several times a year would be cheaper than carrying a seaman all the time. Gordon even had a plan to magnetise the mooring procedure which would pull the vessel into a dock so there was no rope, and so no need for a seaman to throw it.

Apart from trying to convince the Seamens Union, Gordon Barton needed government approval and support to get the finance. Gordon Barton called on Prime Minister Fraser, and his Transport Minister Peter Nixon, and obtained their in-principle support. Gordon and Ken Thomas met the Victorian and Tasmanian premiers and they too liked the idea. The London financiers wanted assurances of the support of the Tasmanian Government, and asked for them to guarantee $15 million, half of the loan. This required legislation, and when that was done it made the plan look a certainty. While the ships could be built overseas at a lower price, Barton wanted to have them built in Australia, and there was a ship building subsidy to help.

All these things happening took time and the Seamens Union had used that time to make a big issue of the plan. So the Tasmanian Government lost its nerve and withdrew its support of the concept.

As Ken said to his audience of transport men in Perth, "The people, (meaning the Tasmanians) who had most to gain, were those who destroyed the plan."

Ken despaired that the visionary plan was thwarted because of the narrow outlook of unions and governments.

The concluding words in his address were:

"Clearly the re-establishment of coastal shipping in the non-bulk trades is crucial to an ideal system in this, the island continent. But it has no chance until the labour situation is determined by the government, and not by a group of monopolistic unions who own the exclusive right to work the ship, the wharves or the docks."

Ken gave careful consideration to an invitation to join the board of Qantas. Qantas was at this time fully owned by the Federal Government, so it was the Minister for Transport who appointed the directors, suitable people to run the airline. Ken's extensive experience was recognised, and he would have been a big help in the boardroom.

After some thought Ken decided he had had enough of big business, he preferred the personal touch found in small business, so he declined the offer.

THE LATER YEARS

After his dismissal in 1972 Ken Thomas had to decide his future course. He had just celebrated his 59th birthday, he was in good health, and in the public eye because of the success of TNT and his stance on different causes. Ken was not the sort of man who could sit at home for the rest of his life. Financially he was in good shape as he had made money and owned property. Being involved in other businesses appealed to him, and there were entrepreneurs who wanted Ken's support.

For 25 years Ken had had a special love of Far North Queensland. Now there would be more time to enjoy this passion.

The meeting of Keith Hollands at Murwillumbah, back in 1956 had proved to be a real milestone. Keith had given a lot of thought to the transport needs of this part of Australia, and suggested to Ken that there was a need for small ships to run from Cairns to Cape York, and the Torres Islands, and into the Gulf of Carpentaria. Ken has seen the sense of this, and they had formed a company, Keith Hollands Shipping Co Pty Ltd. Ken was the Chairman, and Keith the Managing Director.

Top: *The Katoora, was the second ship bought by Keith Hollands Shipping. It was built in Scotland in 1925, for Australian coastal work. She was for sale in 1960 because the new bulk sugar terminals had meant there was no longer a need for sugar lighters to take bagged sugar out to overseas ships. With a length of 120 feet, she could carry 400 tons.*

Bottom: *The Maluka, right, and Kattoora, being loaded at Cairns. With no mechanical equipment, the ship's crew had to man handle the drums of distillate.*

In 1958 they found a ship under construction at Woodburn on the Richmond River, in northern NSW. The builder had run out of money so accepted an offer of £ 30,000. The vessel was completed, launched and named the 'Maluka. On the 9th May 1959 she arrived in Cairns ready to start a new service. This caused quite a stir as John Burke Ltd had been operating their ships in this area for sixty years, and dominated the industry. A competitor was not welcome.

Ken flew to Cairns for the maiden voyage with Keith to Torres Strait. They had decided two principles. Firstly to avoid Union problems they would not use the normal waterside workers to handle the cargo. Secondly to provide a regular and reliable service, the Maluka would sail fortnightly, while John Burke only ran eleven trips each year. Fortunately Keith Hollands had picked up the business of Mobil Oil, Mobil supplied the majority of the fuel used in Torres Strait, which was carried in 44 gallon drums. In about six months there was sufficient business to warrant another ship, so the Katoora joined the fleet. The ships serviced the various ports and settlements from Cooktown up to Thursday Island and the other islands. When Comalco started mining at Weipa on the western side of the Cape, the service was extended to there. The Queensland Government had for years nominated a carrier for all the Government freight to this area and Keith Hollands won that business from John Burke.

Ken and Keith had from the start recruited Torres Strait Islanders for their crew. They usually had seven of these experienced seafarers on each ship, five on board while two had shore leave. The crew did the loading and unloading, but in Cairns this had to be done away from the main wharves where the Waterside Workers Union ruled the roost. Ken and Keith managed to find a private wharf on Smiths Creek.

Top: *The Cairns wharf used had been built during the War, and no longer in good condition. It was known as the cannery wharf because there had been a pineapple cannery behind the wharf. Using this wharf allowed non union, Torres Strait crew to handle the cargo.*

Bottom: *On board the Maluka. Ken Thomas, 2nd from right, and Keith Hollands on right with a tie. Rhody Thomas, then a teenager on extreme left.*

Above: The completed dry dock, it was the first in North Queensland.

The continuing problem was back loading. They did find some high grade tin ore to take to Cairns and was then sent by rail to Sunnymount, hundreds of kilometres west of Cairns. There was some sawn timber to go south from the Cape, and fish was picked up and carried in freezer boxes.

Early in the 1960s the road system in the Cape York area was virtually non-existent. There was no coast road to Cooktown, so ships were the vital means of transport. The ships did go across the Gulf of Carpentaria to Normanton, Karumba, Burketown and Mornington Island. However the volume of cargo going to these places was quite small. When offered the Government contract Keith Hollands proposed that it go by road from Cairns, via Croydon to Normanton to the gulf, and by sea from there. The road across Western

Queensland was no more than two wheel tracks, and holdups were frequent but they did pioneer a service.gradually the road was upgraded, particularly by the Federal Government's beef roads scheme, and road transport became more feasible. Other road carriers of course joined in.

Keith Hollands Shipping even extended to New Guinea. In 1966 the company announced that Jardine, their new ship built in Cairns would run to Daru, a small island in the estuary of the Fly River. There were plans to backload with fish, particularly Barramundi, which would then go south from Cairns by road. The Jardine was a sister ship of the ' Kennedy' another ship the company owned and was being used to serve the ports on the Gulf.

To operate a fleet of ships means there has to be a dry dock available for repairs and the annual survey, and as there was no dock in Cairns, Ken Thomas and Keith Hollands decided that they should build one, so formed a company Cairns Dry Dock and Engineering. The dock was completed in April 1967, and the second 'Maluka' was the first ship to use it. The Australian Navy was pleased to see the dock and moved the base of the RAN Patrol boats from Townsville to Cairns to facilitate their use of the new dock.

Keith Hollands Shipping owned and operated the dock until 1975 when it was sold to Wm. Angliss who needed a dock for their prawn trawlers

The gradual building of a road north from Cooktown, to serve Weipa and then on to the tip of the Cape, allowed road transport to service Torres Strait as well. Keith Hollands wound down slowly.

At its peak the company owned and operated six ships and employed about 100 people.

Top: *The dredge, Trinty Bay, improving access to the dock.*

Bottom: *The Maluka 2, approaching the new dock. She was the first ship to use the dock.*

There was also an airline, Queensland Pacific Airways (QPA), which owned a number of DC3 cargo planes. It was the third largest-heavy airline in Australia, next after Ansett and TAA. QPA had success with carrying fruit and vegetables to Torres Strait, and returning with prawns. Ken's son Rhody was also involved with some of these ventures.

The Gulf of Carpentaria was the location of the prawn trawler fishing operation, with a 'mother ship' and about six trawlers. The 'mother ship', with a crew of two women circulated round the trawlers to collect and freeze their catch, then deliver it to the port. A mystery arose as to why the collection round was taking so long. The answer emerged, the women were also providing 'other services' for the men, which took the time.

Then there were other mining ventures: gold mining in Queensland and Victoria, and sapphire mining in New South Wales.

In 1977, Ken was a director and substantial shareholder in nine different companies. They all had problems and Ken lost money.

There was even a return to transport. Tenex was born. This was a venture with son Rhody for an express road service to North Queensland. The name came from the objective of being able to deliver to the consignees by 10am each day. The company had four trucks and ran mainly between Cairns and Mackay, with connections to Brisbane. Ken was featured in a story in *The Australian*, complete with his photo saying the intention was to expand the service to Sydney, Melbourne and Adelaide. That did not happen, and as the business was not doing well, Ken asked his old mate Gordon Barton to buy Tenex, so he could be rid of it. Tenex was absorbed into IPEC.

As a well-known businessman, Ken was invited to become a director and chairman of Oceanic Equity, a property trust. This was a new form of investment, where there are shares in a particular property or group of properties. The investors would get their dividends from the rental income and the value of the shares increase as the property appreciates.

Road safety had been a concern that worried Ken for years. His eldest daughter, Elizabeth, had suffered from a bad car accident in 1970, in which she was thrown from the car driven by her husband. Her survival was a miracle and she still carried injuries. There were a number of his employees and contractors, many of whom Ken knew personally, who had been killed or injured in road accidents.

One of the reasons why he so strongly advocated rail was that it decreased the number of trucks on the road. That made the road a safer place.

Ken had established a good relationship with Milton Morris, the Minister for Transport in the New South Wales Liberal Government, led by Rob Askin. They had much in common to discuss as Milton was from a three generation railway family. Milton loved trains and admired Ken's enthusiasm for their role in the transport task. The two men shared an interest in the Central Methodist Mission as they were both active supporters and met at Mission board meetings.

Milton Morris served as the transport minister for 10 years from 1965, still a record term for that portfolio in New South Wales history. Transport was to most politicians a 'poisoned chalice' as the Minister copped the blame for all the problems. Milton was different; he had his eye on that job since he entered parliament in 1956, so was well prepared for it.

Ken Thomas became a very strong advocate for seatbelts in road vehicles. The Snowy Mountain Authority (SMA) was the first organisation in Australia to fit seatbelts to all their vehicles. In the 1950s, they were building the Snowy Mountains Scheme with dams and power stations in rugged and mountainous country, with poor roads. Employees had to use the seatbelts and it did reduce the road accident fatalities. Ken knew this and he discussed it with Milton Morris.

Milton described Ken as "A true leader in the transport industry who has not been recognised as he should be." Milton in retirement remembers Ken most for his work in road safety. Ken's influence was a major factor in his decision in 1971 to make seatbelts compulsory in New South Wales. There was considerable opposition from the public, but there is no doubt that seatbelts did make a big difference to the fatality figures.

Even with seatbelts, road accident figures in the late 1970s were still too high and growing each year. In 1978 there were 1384 deaths on New South Wales roads; like most people Ken was appalled, but unlike most people Ken decided to do something more about it.

The Liberal Government had been defeated in 1975 so Ken had to convince a Labor Government with Neville Wran as premier. To Ken's dismay they showed little interest in the problem.

While it was easy enough to express dismay to a politician, the problem needed practical suggestions about what to do. Ken's answer was to rally concerned people into an organisation and gather support. The gathering of numbers is always the best way to attract the attention of politicians.

SALAD was formed, ('Save A Life A Day') and Ken started looking for members. He managed to find some unused office space, available for free at Reiby Place in the city, then recruited some women prepared to work as unpaid volunteers. Ken of course paid all the expenses, particularly advertising and printing.

SALAD's platform was to adopt the road safety methods that were working in Victoria.

Victoria had achieved a downturn in accident rates, so that was a good model for New South Wales. In Victoria, road safety was the responsibility of the Minister for Police and Emergency Services. This made sense as the police force attend all accidents and knew what is happening on the roads. Ken was convinced that alcohol was the root of the problem. But Aussies like to drink, and anything to curb that was going to be unpopular.

In 1976 Victoria had introduced random breath testing at road blocks and of all drivers involved in accidents.

SALAD maintained that the penalties for drink driving were not high enough in New South Wales and needed to be increased. Driver training in high schools was another Victorian practice.

Enforcement was important. If police and courts were not taking tough action with offenders, and the penalties were too low, the message was not getting to drivers. SALAD advocated that drunk drivers should be gaoled.

Ken proposed that local accident figures should be highlighted, to gain attention and build a desire to reduce the accident rate. That meant that road safety efforts should be decentralised, and not all be controlled from Sydney.

There was a need for a target figure to reduce accidents. Limit 18 was suggested by SALAD; 18 being the target maximum number of road deaths per week in the state, a total of 936 for the year. This was still too high, but an achievable target in the first year.

To the best of Ken's knowledge, SALAD was the only private organisation fighting for New South Wales road safety, otherwise the effort was being left to public servants and politicians.

Ken appointed some interested people to a committee, but he remained the convenor. Appeals were made for members and donations, with memberships starting at $1. People were asked to work in their own neighbourhood to arouse awareness and financial support. All money raised was being spent on advertising.

Naturally Ken used his contacts to get publicity and succeeded in getting newspaper space.

The *Sydney Morning Herald* of 24th March 1979 had a half-page story headed SALAD MAKES A SOLID START. There was a large photo of Ken, with the caption, *Ken Thomas crusading against road deaths.* There were figures on the way the membership was growing, and people were contributing money. About 300 people had written making good sensible suggestions about road safety.

The story pointed out that the saving of lives was paramount, but a reduction in the accident rate also meant there was a considerable saving in the costs of medical care to injured victims, and the costs of repairs and write-offs of damaged vehicle. Car insurance premiums would go down if there were fewer accident claims. A saving of $1 million per day was estimated.

The Victorian record of saving lives was the constant theme. Victoria a few years earlier had more accidents than New South Wales, although the Victorian

AN OPEN LETTER TO NEVILLE WRAN Q.C.

FROM THE SALAD MOVEMENT
To Save-A-Life-A-Day in New South Wales

2nd Floor, Reiby Chambers,
27 Reiby Place, Sydney 2000
Phone 233 7971

Dear Mr. Premier,

IF YOUR GOVERNMENT were to adopt Victoria's road safety methods we would save more than one life a day in New South Wales.

COMPARATIVE FIGURES for the two States up to 8th September this year show that if we matched Victoria's results pro rata to population we would save 410 lives a year.

AS COMPARED WITH LAST YEAR road deaths in N.S.W. would come down from 1290 to 880, a reduction of 32%. Add to this an equivalent reduction in victims injured and permanently maimed, some of them suffering a life worse than death. In crude money terms, the saving would be over $1 million a day.

IT IS NOT MERELY a matter of adopting Victoria's methods of random road-block breath testing. Nothing less than their entire road safety organisation and controls will suffice.

WE REQUEST you to answer the following questions as though they were 'questions with notice' in the House:—

1. Will your government adopt in its entirety the system of road safety organisation and control as practised in Victoria?
2. In particular, will you transfer the entire responsibility for road safety control **and research** to a Minister for Police and Emergency Services, as in Victoria?
3. As President of the Australian Labor Party, do you consider that the need to **raise the standard** of road safety in New South Wales should be a major issue in the forthcoming Federal election?

SALAD will be pleased to publish your reply to this letter.

Yours sincerely,

Ken Thomas.

Convener,
The SALAD
(Save-A-Life-A-Day) Movement.

WE NEED FUNDS

to sustain political pressure for adoption of our complete road safety programme.

The Secretary,
The Salad Movement.
Box 79 G.P.O.
Sydney 2001

Please forward a copy of the
Road Safety Prospectus
I enclose
$1—membership fee
$5—annual fee for 1980
$ donation for advertising

We are an entirely voluntary organisation, we pay no salaries and our City office is provided rent free by the Hooker Corporation. Every dollar you give is used effectively.

Name

Address

Authorised by K. W. Thomas 27 Reiby Place, Sydney, NSW, 2000.

The SALAD ad, letter to Wran.

257

population was less, and with fewer cars. As a result of their activities, the accident rate was now less than in New South Wales.

Ken collected information and statistics from other countries, and frequently measured NSW against other places. Any chance he had to promote road safety was utilised. In a talk he told a tale against himself.

"In Cairns, some years ago I committed an offence, and drove across a railway line without stopping. A policeman saw me, and swooped. After a severe lecture, he said he would let me off with a warning. His closing shot hit me between the eyes, when he said, "We are proud of our safety record in Cairns, and we don't like you southerners coming up here and spoiling it."

Ken observed, "There were three elements in that lesson. Firstly he knew the local figures and that Cairns had a better safety record than Townsville and Toowoomba.

Then he was a citizen of Cairns and proud of his city, and thirdly he enabled me to emerge from the dressing down a better driver."

Ken spent much of his time from 1979 to 1981 working on SALAD. Another way to get action on road safety was to have candidates in parliament. For the New South Wales state elections on 19th September 1981, SALAD selected candidates to contest six seats. Ken stood for the seat of Willoughby, which included Castlecrag. None of the SALAD nominees won their seat.

George Paciullo, a Labor MP in the New South Wales Government became convinced and was a strong advocate within the Labor Party for action. In December 1982 RBT (random breath testing) was introduced in New South Wales and accident rates were reduced. In 1983 Ken claimed some credit for his efforts that saw the New South Wales road toll reduced to 670 deaths for the year; an average of 12.8 per week.

By 2012, 85 million breath tests had been taken over 30 years; and the death rate for the year on the roads in New South Wales was down to 370. Thousands of lives have been saved.

Ken's other major interest in retirement was reform of the structure of Australian government. For a long time the current arrangement had irked him. He argued that the state boundaries had just been drawn in London as lines on a map, by men who had never been to Australia, and the states were just the area around a settlement made by the original colonists. He thought these boundaries were completely irrelevant to good government in Australia in the 20th century.

Ken was also strong on decentralisation, and the need for local people to be better able to govern themselves.

Power to the people was his constant theme. Frequently Ken recalled a speech by Sir Robert Menzies, who as prime minister had said "The role of government was to administer, not to create." This Ken said, "left open who was to lead. If the politicians would not, the public servants would not, so leadership is left to the people. However, most of the general public were badly informed, not interested or only looking after their own interests."

Ken saw the need for leadership, and he thought the best way to get that is to start close to home, the local scene.

Ken spent a lot of time dreaming and talking about a new structure, and that would mean a new Australian Constitution. His plan varied over the years from the early 1970s to the 1990s. In that time he published several pamphlets and books, and distributed them widely. Naturally he sent them to the federal and state politicians and local councils Australia wide. Ken loved it when he received a reply, arguing about some of his proposals. Ken was disgusted when he was ignored, or had a polite note of acknowledgement and nothing more. However he did build up an impressive number of people with whom he corresponded, in some cases for years as they debated and found fault and the good points of Ken's ideas.

One frequent correspondent was retired senator Jim McClelland. Jim had a column in the *Sydney Morning Herald* every week, and Ken read that closely then often sent a letter of protest or congratulations to Jim. John Button was another retired senator who corresponded regularly and commented on Ken's plan.

The last book Ken produced was in December 1994. It had 66 pages and was titled

"REGIONAL GOVERNMENT"
A PLAN FOR PARLIAMENTARY REFORM

Ken had formed TARGA (The Australian Regional Government Association). The introduction to the book said, *"The TARGA concept has the potential to become a ground swell of public opinion by the turn of the century."*

The book was critical of the current situation and detailed the problems.

Ken's solution was the abolition of the state governments and their replacement with 37 regional governments. Each of them would have much the same responsibilities as the state governments now had. People would vote for their regional councillors, and one of the councillors would be nominated as the senator for that region. The senate would sit in Canberra and be the Federal Government responsible for national matters, such as defence, foreign affairs and international trade. All other matters would be the responsibility of the regional council.

Ken hated the adversarial system that resulted from political parties confronting each other and trying to belittle the ideas and activities of each other. He wanted a system where all the politicians worked together in harmony for the good of the country.

Using census statistics, the book illustrated the proposed 37 regions. While Ken's original idea was they should all have roughly the same population, it became apparent that was not practical, taking into account the big variation in population density in Australia. So a weighted voting system in the senate was proposed, meaning a senator from a region with a larger population would have more voting power than a senator for a smaller region. Ken took as a model the system of shareholders voting at a company meeting. The number of votes each shareholder has equals the number of shares owned.

In the plan that Ken drew there was still a need for local councils, and the plan said they should be close to the people and the smaller the better. There was no suggested limit to the number of local councils in a region.

The book said very little about finance or where the regions would get their money, and where the decisions would be made about public spending.

Ken kept going with TARGA, and in 1995 said, "TARGA is an aberration,that keeps what's left of my marbles active. It entails a certain amount of correspondence and has a reasonable chance of succeeding in the medium term of 20 years. Everyone tells me it is too radical, but nevertheless it is gathering support. No one has yet told me what is wrong with the concept."

The last business Ken was involved in was in a completely different area: rubber rollers. The rollers are used in industry for printing and processing various products. Rhody wanted to buy an operating business and asked Ken to help financially.

Neither of them realised what they were buying, as they were apparently misled by an American company whose techniques and equipment were involved. When Rhody was in trouble with it, Ken came into help, and became the managing director. There was tension in the arrangements and some loss of staff when employees defected to the opposition and took customers with them. It was not a happy experience for Ken; the roller business did keep going for 15 years, but Ken made little or no money from this venture.

Ken's finances were in a bad way, and it became necessary in 1986 to sell the family home at Castlecrag. After 47 years that was a blow to all the family. Ken and Anne moved in with their eldest daughter, Elizabeth.

Although it was 15 years since he left the TNT boardroom Ken kept in touch with many of his friends and colleagues, and took a keen interest in what was happening, particularly in Australia. In 1987, Ken was invited to open a new building in Mascot on the site of an earlier TNT building.

The consultancy fee of $35,000 a year from TNT that Ken had negotiated after his dismissal kept coming. There was some hesitation by the board, but Ken maintained it was a lifetime arrangement, and he needed the money. TNT covered the costs of a trip to Europe in 1988 by Ken and Anne.

Gordon Barton was then living in the north of Italy with his son and daughter, while his wife preferred to live in London. Ken arranged to spend a few days with Gordon to talk over old times. At the house, Anne found a bag belonging to Gordon, containing sex toys and fetish clothing. She was so disgusted that she told Ken she would not stay in the house, and demanded their travel arrangements be changed and they leave immediately.

Ken and Anne went on to the United Kingdom. It was 20 years since Ken had been to England, and he was keen to see the TNT operations and meet some of the staff. Ken was welcomed by Alan Jones, Managing Director of TNT in the UK. By that time there were about 2500 TNT trucks in the UK, and 7300 employees.

Ken was interviewed by some UK journalists, and *Commercial Motor* magazine headlined the interview story with:

WIZARD FROM OZ.

It went on to describe him: *"Thomas is everybody's idea of what an Aussie entrepreneur should be, amicable, earthy, and quick with an anecdote, he resembles a character from Neville Shute."*

The story went on to outline Ken's career and tell of the way he had led and shaken up the Australian transport industry in building TNT.

Ken also took up invitations to renew friendships with transport executives in England whom he had met or had contact with over the years.

Back in Harden, his birthplace, Ken was not forgotten. One evening in 1989, young Darren Sergent was told by a friend as they had a drink in the Harden Country Club, "That is Ken Thomas over there," and pointed out a lonely figure finishing a meal. Darren knew a lot about Ken, and his record in the transport industry, so Ken was a hero. As Ken rose to leave, Darren asked could they have a talk.

"No," said Ken, "I am going to the motel now and will be leaving early in the morning."

"Could I talk to you at the motel ?" Darren asked.

"I will be leaving at 6am, so it would have to be before that."

"I am an early riser too," said the persistent Darren, "so I can be there before six."

At ten minutes to six the next morning, Darren arrived at the motel. There was Ken, bag in hand ready to go. "You can drive me down the town," Ken said. "There are a couple of houses I would like to drive past."

They paused at Ken's grandmother Julia's house in Iris street, and then his parent's house in Clarke street. Darren remembers that although it was 17 years since his dismissal from the company, Ken was still bitter about it.

In 1991, Ken lost his beloved Anne, when she died of breast cancer.

Things got very difficult for TNT, and in 1993 Peter Abeles had been sacked from the board of directors. His successor as managing director was David Mortimer, who had been the financial director for some years. Ken wrote to David and said, *"In my opinion you will prove to be much more successful in pulling TNT out of trouble than Peter Abeles. You are a decent Australian, whereas Peter is a devious Hungarian."*

Ken received a letter from Gordon Barton in 1995. Gordon was still living in Italy and they had not been in touch with each other for some years. Gordon had experienced many ups and downs in his business and personal life.

In his reply Ken said, *"It is extraordinary that both of us did well in interstate transport, but failed badly in other ventures. The main thing is we have both held together apart from your hearing problems."* (Barton was by then deaf.)

Ken never lost his interest in the activities of TNT and the employees. David Gronow remembered that he drove Ken to a Comet/Kwikasair gathering in April 1996. Ken was interested in David's role and his background and then asked, "Are we treating our people well in the company?" David found the energy and enthusiasm that Ken showed at age 83 was extraordinary, and had no doubt that was the secret of Ken's success in building TNT.

October 1996 brought some bad news for Ken. The TNT board had resolved to accept the offer to sell the company to KPN, the Dutch Post Office and Telephone Communications group. Ken told Leonie Lamont, a journalist at the *Sydney Morning Herald*, *"The whole takeover is a shameful disgrace. It is another case of selling out an Australian company."*

Ken told Leonie about the Federal Government blocking the sale in 1966 to a UK company, when an offer was made for TNT. *"It was not in the national interest then for the company to be sold, and I believe that still applies. It is an Australian company that has a proud history. It did an enormous job in employing Australians, and set a very, very, high standard of service."*

Ken was in a reminiscent mood, and told her, *"I did not resign from TNT, I was sacked. Freddy Millar wanted to be chairman. He did not want this truckie being chairman. I am a very down to earth person, and suspicious of all forms of ostentation. They usually go with superficial people, especially in the business world. I was never accepted in the business establishment. I said the wrong things, and occasionally did the wrong thing."*

Leonie concluded her story, *"For a man who put trucking on the map, Thomas said his biggest contribution to TNT had been pioneering the use of container transport on the railways."*

In 1994 Ken's sister Julia died and he scored an inheritance of $190,000, from her estate. He decided this was his chance to go bush. Ken was still a country boy, still had the love of the peace and space of rural life. He liked country people as he "found them more civilised than city slickers." So he started looking.

Early in 1995, Ken found a seven-acre block at Tarana. This is a small settlement, with a railway station on the main western line. It had been the junction of the branch line to Oberon 24km south. Tarana is a very pleasant and quiet spot, with Bathurst 35km to the west.

Ken had a plan drawn for a modest two-bedroom brick cottage of about 10 squares (approx 100m²). There was in addition a 3m-wide verandah all round. He called the property 'Skye', after the Scottish island from where his great-grandfather had migrated to Australia. Ken intended to live there alone, but told his friends there was a spare bedroom for visitors. His agriculture experience made him cautious, but an organic garden was on the cards.

Ken had never in his whole life lived alone. Cooking and housekeeping were something he had never had to do. There had always been a mother, a wife or a loving daughter to do those things. Now his two daughters living in Sydney were apprehensive about how it would go. The Tarana Hotel was only a few

THE LAST DINNER

Then managing director, David Mortimer wrote in 2013:

"I invited all surviving directors to the dinner and took the opportunity to invite Ken Thomas and ask him to give an address. He agreed to do this.

I made a speech, and in that speech acknowledged some of the ground breaking initiatives Ken had implemented in his time as leader of the group. Ken was grateful and gracious to me but the devil in him could not be contained. Ken had a 'secret' desire to pour water on those who he saw had abandoned him. Sir Peter was not there that evening, so Fred Millar, his successor as chairman, copped the brunt of Ken's frustrations held for so many years.

Ken was extremely creative and surprisingly well before his time. Several of his initiatives, including some of his HR initiatives and rail consolidation initiatives live on today and are a constant reminder of his excellence."

hundred metres up the road, and a meal there each night was an option. Ken stocked the pantry cupboard with baked beans; he could make a meal with tea and toast of them.

Probably the last contact Ken had with any of the TNT staff was a dinner on 18th February 1997. The invitation said it was to mark the retirement of the Board of Directors of TNT Ltd and to commemorate the company's 50 years of service in Australia.

The board was no longer required because of the split up and sale of TNT. The TNT companies engaged in general cartage by rail and road were to be sold to Toll, and the companies offering fast freight, express services, by road and air were kept, to be controlled from the United Kingdom. So it was all over; Ken's handiwork was dismantled. At the dinner, Ken refused the request made of him to propose a toast, nor would he cut the cake. He was too devastated for that.

In September 1997 Ken was in the process of moving in to his new house. He took a load of possessions up from Sydney, and after arriving felt ill. Ken went to a neighbour who he had befriended and asked for an Aspirin. The friend drove Ken to the doctor at Oberon, who decided that Ken should be hospitalised at Bathurst. The hospital there felt that Orange Base Hospital was better equipped to help, so another ambulance trip was called for.

The staff at Orange had grave fears for him and summoned the family from Sydney. They managed to be there before Ken died on 21st September, aged 84 years and three months. On the death certificate, the doctor gave aortic aneurism as the cause.

Ken's funeral was on 26th September 1997 at the Northern Suburbs Crematorium at North Ryde. The family who gathered that day to remember and honour him were siblings Jean and Ross, his children, Elizabeth, Rhody, Megan and Gavin, and grandchildren, Sean, Seamus, Sam, Sally, Benjamin, Sean, Joshua, Sandy, Tom, Ellen, Laura and Jenni; then two great-grandchildren, Joshua and Isobel.

They had much to be very proud of.

DEATHS

THOMAS, Kenneth William. —
September 21, 1997, at Orange,
late of Castlecrag, dearly beloved
and loved husband of Anne
(deceased), loved father of
Elizabeth, Rhody, Megan, Gavin
and Andrew (deceased), dearly
loved grandfather and great-
grandfather of their children.

Do not go gentle into that good
night.
Aged 84 years.

KENNETH'S family and friends
are invited to attend his funeral
service, to be held in the North
Chapel of the Northern Suburbs
Crematorium, Dehli Road, North
Ryde, commencing at 11.30 a.m.
on Friday (September 26, 1997).

NORMAN J. PENHALL
FUNERALS, F.D.A. (N.S.W.)
William Street, Orange.
Phone (02) 6362 3751.

THE SYDNEY MORNING HERALD
TUESDAY, SEPTEMBER 23, 1997

Ken Thomas
1913 – 1997

KEN THOMAS passed away peacefully last Sunday, at
Orange, New South Wales.

The Management and staff of TNT Australia both past and
present extend their deepest sympathy to his children,
Elizabeth, Megan, Gavin and Rhody and their families on the
very sad loss of their father and grandfather.

All of us at TNT owe a great deal to Ken Thomas. His
contribution to the Company he founded and loved was
immeasurable. He was an inspirational leader, a man of wisdom
and vision, a caring human being and a friend to everyone.

Above all else, he was a great Australian and will be sadly
missed by us all.

The Management & Staff

TNT Australia

T N T Australia

LATER YEARS

Ken and Anne Thomas in London 1988. A long way from the Australian bush.

Ken at a TNT UK depot.

Ken takes a ride in the UK.

Ken Thomas and Peter Abeles.

Top: Ken and Anne Thomas, July 1989

Bottom: Brian Bertwistle and Ken Thomas enjoy each others company, July 1989

Joan and Ken Smith with Ken Thomas.

David Mortimer and Fred Millar at the 'Last Dinner'.

A TNT road train in the Northern Territory. Before the opening of the rail line between Alice Springs and Darwin in 2004, road transport was the life line for Darwin and the Top End.

TRIBUTES TO KEN THOMAS

Transport pioneer Thomas dead at 84

Mr Ken Thomas, one of Australia's most colourful postwar industrial pioneers and a founder of the international transport conglomerate, TNT Ltd, has died at the age of 84.

He was absorbed with business right up to the end, cutting his final deal just two weeks ago with the sale of the Sydney operations of the family's rubber-roller group, Rollmakers Australia.

It was typical of the so-called "educated truckie", who emerged through sheer hard work and corporate guile to play a significant role in the development of the nation's transport industry.

He also established himself as a prominent social conscience, fighting against the Vietnam War in the 1960s and heading a campaign in NSW that led to the introduction of random breath testing for drivers.

But Mr Thomas is best known for laying the foundations for the creation of the TNT trucking goliath by negotiating a merger between his company, Thomas Nationwide Transport, and Sir Peter Abeles' Alltrans group in 1967.

He departed as chairman of TNT five years later – a move he blamed on his successor, Mr Fred Millar – but continued to be actively involved in a broad range of business activities until his death.

Mr Thomas's son, Gavin, yesterday buried long-held rumours of ill feeling

Mr Thomas was absorbed with business to the end. Picture: ANDREW TAYLOR

between his father and Sir Peter, saying: "There was no animosity. Peter Abeles and dad were friends and had a healthy liking and respect for each other."

He said that his father had orchestrated the merger with Alltrans to secure the highly regarded services of Sir Peter and his management team.

However, he confirmed that Mr Ken Thomas – like Sir Peter – was bitterly opposed to the $2 billion takeover of TNT late last year by the Dutch postal and

telecommunications group KPN. "He felt that the Australian management had sold out. It was an Australian company and Australian jobs would be lost as a result of the takeover," Mr Gavin Thomas, one of Mr Thomas's four surviving children, said.

Mr Thomas died on Sunday night at the seven-acre country retreat he was building him in western NSW. A service will be held for him at 11.30am on Friday at the Northern Suburbs crematorium in Sydney.

271

C 2   THE AGE MONDAY 6 OCTOBER 1997

MET

Obituaries

Unsung hero a truckie at heart

Ken Thomas

Former chairman of Thomas
Nationwide Transport
Born: 1913
Died: 21 September 1997, aged 84

IT STARTED as a one-truck general haulage operation. But Ken Thomas saw it grow into Thomas Nationwide Transport (TNT), an international business empire moving freight on four continents.

"Trucking is in my bones. I have always thought of myself as a truckie," Thomas observed. Yet, he was also an astute and fearless innovator, who became one of the captains of post-war Australian industry.

A man with sound commercial ambitions, Thomas's social, religious and political views often put him at odds with most of his corporate peers as well as Australian governments. At various times, he spoke out loudly against organised religion, the Liberal Party, the Vietnam War and, indeed, Australia's entire system of government.

He also headed a campaign in New South Wales that eventually led to the introduction of random breath testing of drivers.

While other business leaders of his generation duly collected awards for services to industry or to the community, Thomas remained undecorated. Asked why he had never been offered a knighthood, he offered a succinct reply: "Because the Government knows I would never accept one of their honors . . . and they don't want to risk the embarrassment of my refusal."

Although he had severed his connection with TNT — resigning as chairman in 1983 — Thomas continued to devote his talents to a wide range of business activities almost right up to his death.

Kenneth William Thomas was born in Harden, NSW, the son of an engine driver, and educated at the local school. He began work as a bank officer, found it unsatisfying for his restless temperament and gave it up for other jobs, including car salesman, personnel officer and clerk. He graduated with arts and economics degrees from Sydney University, studying part-time.

Twenty years after buying his first truck, Thomas negotiated a merger between his company and Sir Peter Abeles' Alltrans Group, but gave up the chairmanship of the company in 1972.

He continued to be widely respected as a wise corporate manager and a caring employer.

Thomas died at his country property in western NSW. His wife, Anne, predeceased him. He is survived by his children, Elizabeth, Megan, Gavin and Rhody, and grandchildren.

— James Cunningham

Saturday, September 27, 1997

OBITUARIES

Ken Thomas

1913 – 1997

It was, to start with, only a one-truck general haulage operation. But Ken Thomas, who has died at 84, saw it grow into Thomas Nationwide Transport (TNT), an international business empire moving freight on four continents.

"Trucking is in my bones. I have always thought of myself as a truckie," Thomas once observed. Yet he was also an astute and fearless innovator who became one of the outstanding captains of post-war Australian industry.

Surprisingly for a man with such sound commercial ambitions, Thomas's social, religious and political views often put him at odds with most of his corporate peers as well as Australian governments. At various times he spoke out loudly against organised religion, the Liberal Party, the Vietnam War and, indeed, Australia's entire system of government. He also headed a campaign in NSW that eventually led to the introduction of random breath testing for drivers.

Noticeably, while other business leaders of his generation duly collected awards for services to industry or to the community, Thomas remained undecorated. And in reply to a question on one occasion as to why he had never been offered a knighthood he offered a succinct reply. "Because the Government knows I would never accept one of their honours . . . and they don't want to risk the embarrassment of my refusal," he explained.

Although he had severed his connection with TNT — resigning as chairman in 1983 — Thomas continued to devote his talents to a wide range of business activities right up, almost, to his death on September 21.

Kenneth William Thomas was born in Harden, NSW, the son of an engine driver, and educated at the local school. He began work as a bank officer, found it unsatisfying for his restless temperament and gave it up for other jobs, including van salesman, personnel officer and clerk. Part-time study led to his graduating with Arts and Economics degrees from Sydney University. Twenty years after buying his first truck, Thomas nego-

tiated a merger between his company and Sir Peter Abeles' Alltrans Group but gave up the chairmanship of the company in 1972. Among his subsequent business interests was an involvement with the rubber roller group, Rollmakers Australia. He continued to be widely respected as a wise corporate manager and a caring employer.

Ken Thomas died at his country property in western NSW. His wife, Anne, predeceased him. He is survived by his children, Elizabeth, Megan, Gavin and Rhody, and grandchildren. A funeral service was held for him in the North Chapel of the Northern Suburbs Crematorium, North Ryde, yesterday.

272

Australia says farewell to a man of great vision

Peter Costigan

ONE of the best and least known Australians died peacefully this week. He was a man who transformed post-war transport across the nation and had those who wield power listened, could have transformed our political and economic map as well.

Ken Thomas was the T in the giant transport company TNT, which he created in the sixties and ran as Thomas National Transport, later expanding it jointly with the legendary Sir Peter Abeles.

Incidentally, Ken's son Gavin this week scotched long circulating rumours that Thomas and Abeles had fallen out after Thomas left the company several years ago. Far from a falling out, they were always good friends and united last year in a vigorous but quixotic effort to stop the Australian-owned TNT being swallowed up by a Dutch transport giant in a $2000 million deal.

Both men tried to stop the deal for one simple reason.

They believed, accurately, that it would cost Australian jobs.

Ken Thomas's name is known to millions of Australians simply because of the impact of his giant transport company and its involvement in the daily movement of so much freight and people (for a long time it was half owner of Ansett Airlines) to every corner of the country.

Under the Thomas plan, which he called FORM (for Federation of Regions' Movement), each of the 37 regional governments would appoint two members to represent it in the 74-member national parliament which, in deference to the Roman rather than the Australian or American tradition, would be called the Senate.

Each regional government, by the way, would have just eight elected members, meaning that Australia would have just less than

area, is divided into seven separate mini States, some of which intrude into parts of the Northern Territory and New South Wales.

The Gold Coast region logically includes Tweed Heads, which is clearly part of the culture and economic entity of the region, but is now part of NSW, not Queensland.

The most densely populated part of Australia, the south-east corner, has the most numerous divisions.

Ken Thomas and his advisors based their research on the 1986 census, but there has been no change in the basic demographics of Australia and his proposals are as valid today as they were when he published them privately in 1992. Our biggest city, Sydney, would be divided into six regions, including parts of the Sydney basin and surrounding areas. Melbourne gets four regions.

But, apart from the logic of his regional arrangements, there is another benefit of the plan for south-east Australia.

It would rid Australia of the artificial nonsense of the so-called rivalry between the two most populous and powerful States.

The areas bordering the Murray River are combined into one region stretching from west of Mildura to east of Holbrook and Corryong, from just south of Broken Hill in the north to just south of Shepparton, Wangaratta and Beechworth.

ACKNOWLEDGEMENTS

Ken Thomas left many papers. They included letters and notes he had written, memos and directions he had sent to his staff and others. There were copies of reports, and letters he received. Ken had intended to write his autobiography, and wrote about his early years. It is not known why he did not complete the task.

Referenced in Chapters 1,2,3,4,5,7,8,9,10,11,12,13,14,15,16

Research on the Thomas & Mcleod families and their life in Harden has been done by Robyn Atherton, a genealogist, and President of the Harden Historical Society.

Referenced in Chapter 1

Ken's son Rhody has many memories of his father and been helpful with information.

Referenced in Chapters 2,3,7,16

Truck & Bus Transportation. Shennan Publishing, a monthly magazine no longer published.

Referenced in Chapters 3,4,5,6,8,9,10

Geoff Hammond's family, daughter Christine and Marleen his second wife, have shared their memories.

Referenced in Chapters 3,12

Ken Smith's family.

Referenced in Chapters 3,12

Darren Sargent of Harden.

Referenced in Chapter 4

ACKNOWLEDGEMENTS

Along Parallel lines. A History of NSW Railways, by John Gunn 1989.

Referenced in Chapters 4,5,6

Railway Transportation. Shennan Publishing, a monthly magazine no longer published.

Referenced in Chapters 5,6,8

Wentworth Report. Commonwealth Government Printer. Nov 1956

Referenced in Chapter 6

From Goods Trains to Freight Logistics: Australian Railways and Container Revolution. Bob McKillop 2012.

Referenced in Chapter 6

Thomas family legend.

Referenced in Chapter 12

Elizabeth Lander, eldest daughter of Ken Thomas.

Referenced in Chapters 7,16

Gavin Thomas, son of Ken Thomas.

Referenced in Chapters 7,16

Bob McKillop, personal recollection.

Referenced in Chapter 7

REFERENCES

Vision Valley brochure.

Referenced in Chapter 7

Max Winkless. Former M.D of Antill Ranger.

Referenced in Chapter 8

Graham Hartman recollection.

Referenced in Chapter 8

Gordon Barton, a biography, by Sam Everingham. 2009.

Referenced in Chapter 11

The Allens Affair, by Valerie Lawson. 1995.

Referenced in Chapter 12

Freight Notes. A TNT staff magazine, published about four times each year.

Referenced in Chapters 12,13,14

Peter Abeles web page.

Referenced in Chapter 12

Track and Signal Magazine. Vol 16, winter 2012.

Referenced in Chapter 12

Ross Hollands, son of Keith Hollands

Referenced in Chapters 8,16

INDEX

278

APPENDIX

PHILOSOPHY OF KEN THOMAS

Ken was a man who had certain principles and guidelines that he used in his personal and business life. He was not hesitant to share them with his family, employees, business associates and audiences who he was invited to address.

- The chief end of man is to glorify the natural world, and enjoy life.

- Without tension there is no creation.

- Do not be afraid of change. Change is vitality, do not resist it.

- In business be "NOT THE BIGGEST, BUT THE BEST." By being the best, a business becomes the biggest. That leads to being most profitable, which can support high salaries and wages, employee benefits and generous dividends to the shareholders.

- To develop the best service it is necessary to develop the best staff and reward them accordingly.

- The results of a year's work are not measured in dollars alone. The contribution to quality of life is another important test, but hard to assess.

- The social responsibility of a business is to give excellent service, and lead in community and social activities relevant to the business. In TNT's case that was the concern for road safety, and helping to reduce accidents, and save lives.

- As Bertrand Russell said: "Be isolated, be ignored, be attacked, be in doubt, be frightened, but do not be silenced. What is important in human experience is intellectual independence, and creative intelligence."

- Be happy, you have to laugh. Through all of life's struggles you have to keep laughing.

APPENDIX B

THOMAS FAMILY TREE

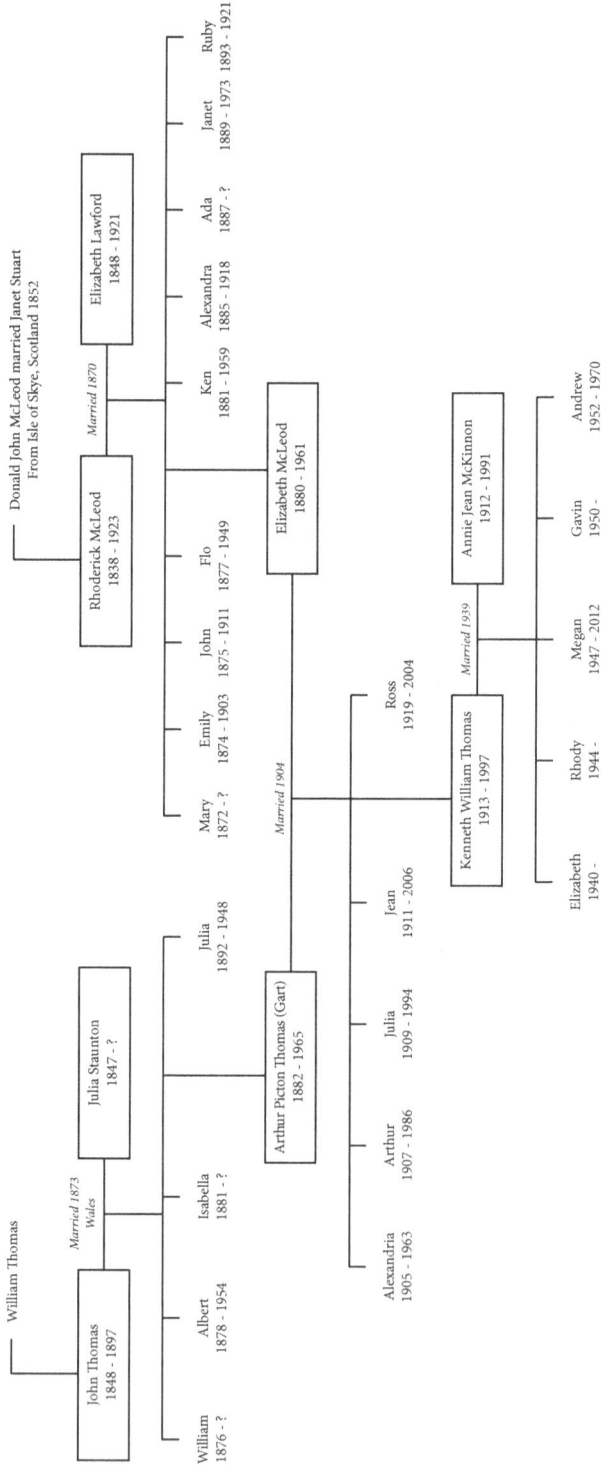

Donald John McLeod married Janet Stuart
From Isle of Skye, Scotland 1852

Married 1870

Rhoderick McLeod
1838 - 1923

Elizabeth Lawford
1848 - 1921

Ken
1881 - 1959

Alexandra
1885 - 1918

Ada
1887 - ?

Janet
1889 - 1973

Ruby
1893 - 1921

Mary
1872 - ?

Emily
1874 - 1903

John
1875 - 1911

Flo
1877 - 1949

Elizabeth McLeod
1880 - 1961

Married 1904

William Thomas

Married 1873
Wales

John Thomas
1848 - 1897

Julia Staunton
1847 - ?

William
1876 - ?

Albert
1878 - 1954

Isabella
1881 - ?

Julia
1892 - 1948

Arthur Picton Thomas (Gart)
1882 - 1965

Alexandria
1905 - 1963

Arthur
1907 - 1986

Julia
1909 - 1994

Jean
1911 - 2006

Ross
1919 - 2004

Kenneth William Thomas
1913 - 1997

Annie Jean McKinnon
1912 - 1991

Married 1939

Elizabeth
1940 -

Rhody
1944 -

Megan
1947 - 2012

Gavin
1950 -

Andrew
1952 - 1970

KEN THOMAS TIMELINES

1913	Born at Harden NSW	1966	Takes active part in opposing Vietnam war
1925	Starts Fort Street High School, Sydney	1967	TNT buys Alltrans
1928	Gains Intermediate Certificate		Visits Vietnam. Stands for election to Senate
1929	Starts work at State Savings Bank		Vietnam debate with Ken Gee
1932	Gains matriculation certificate	1968	Sells Mt Wilson property, buys Palm Beach house
1935	Graduates with Arts degree		
1937	Obtains Economics degree	1969	Establishes "Australian Peace Institute"
1939	Marries Anne McKinnon		
1940-45	Wartime Manpower work for Federal Government		Makes overseas trip with Anne and youngest son, Andrew
1946	Buys truck and starts business	1970	Andrew, Ken's son suicides
1948	Runs business full time Buys Campbell & Landers Pty Ltd		Buys 'Woodleigh' at Narromine
			TNT inaugurates full trains Sydney-Melbourne
1951	Formed K.W.Thomas Transport Pty Ltd		Lobbies NSW Government for compulsory seatbelts
1952	Signs first bulk-loading contract with railways	1972	Dismissed from TNT
1954	Privy Council decides interstate road taxes illegal	1976	Sells 'Woodleigh'
		1979	Forms SALAD
1956	Moves into new terminal at Mascot, Sydney	1981	Contests NSW election as SALAD candidate
1956	Buys holiday house at Mount Wilson	1988	Visits Italy and UK with Anne
1958	Company name becomes TNT. Thomas National Transport Pty Ltd.	1991	Anne dies
		1994	Publishes book with Plan for Regional Government
1961	Company becomes public. TNT. Thomas Nationwide Transport Ltd.		
		1995	Buys land at Tarana
1962	Opening standard gauge Sydney-Melbourne line	1997	Dies at Orange
1964	Starts Comet Overnight Express Pty Ltd.		

GROWTH OF THE BUSINESS

Year	Employees	Trucks	Turnover	Profit	Total Assets
1946	1	1		£120	
1948		4			
1950	18				
1951	32	18			
1955	200	70			
1959		100			
1962			$8.97m	$263,000	$4.05m
1963			$12.25m	$365,000	$5.52m
1964			$15.3m	$502,000	$6.46m
1966	1600	800	$19m	$677,000	$10.83m
1967			$46.7m	$956,243	$23.59m
1968	4,000	3,000	$49.1m	$1.51m	$21.46m
1970			$80.96m	$3.12m	$38.49m
1971			$102m	$3.75m	$45.41m
1972	6,916		$122m	$4.83m	$63.31m

Above and right: 1972 Annual Report: revenue, employees,
associated companies and equipment used

WHERE REVENUE WAS OBTAINED

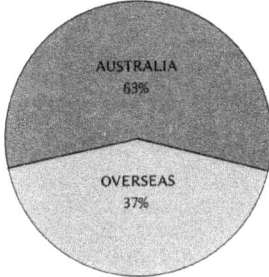

AUSTRALIA 63%

OVERSEAS 37%

HOW EVERY DOLLAR OF CONSOLIDATED REVENUE WAS SPENT

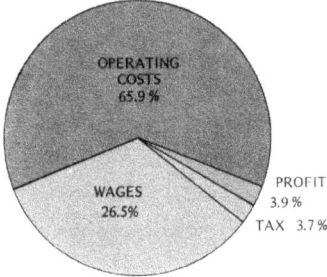

OPERATING COSTS 65.9%

WAGES 26.5%

PROFIT 3.9%

TAX 3.7%

WHERE DID PROFIT GO

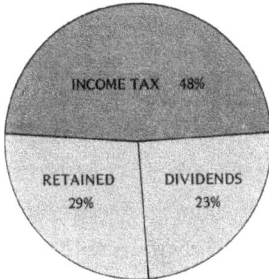

INCOME TAX 48%

RETAINED 29%

DIVIDENDS 23%

NUMBER OF EMPLOYEES WITHIN: TNT GROUP

Australia	5,048
New Zealand	403
U.S.A.	663
Canada	802
TOTAL	6,916

ASSOCIATED COMPANIES

Bulkships Limited & Seatainer Terminals Limited	2,670
Union Steam Ship Company of New Zealand Limited	3,345

TYPES OF EQUIPMENT USED

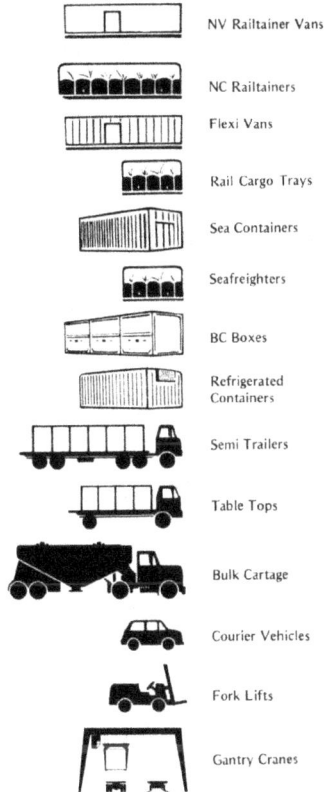

NV Railtainer Vans

NC Railtainers

Flexi Vans

Rail Cargo Trays

Sea Containers

Seafreighters

BC Boxes

Refrigerated Containers

Semi Trailers

Table Tops

Bulk Cartage

Courier Vehicles

Fork Lifts

Gantry Cranes

TNT AFTER KEN THOMAS

After Ken Thomas had left the board of directors, Fred Millar became the chairman. Peter Abeles was the managing director, and was very much in control and so running the company.

That gave Peter the chance to follow his earlier instinct and concentrate on overseas expansion.

The first step was the buying of road transport companies in the United States. There were also purchases in Canada and Brazil. In those countries buying an existing operator was the best way to get a foothold in the industry, but there were many problems with wildcat strikes, arson and even bombings. TNT was handicapped for years by such troubles, apparently because of the resentment of unions and competitor companies.

The next plan was taking on the powerful trans-Atlantic shipping companies, by establishing a non-conference container shipping service, Trans Freight Lines in competition.

An office was established in London and from there operations were established in the United Kingdom and Europe. There was nothing like the overnight express service available in Australia, with Comet and Kwikasair, so TNT tried that. Kwikasair opened a London to Paris operation in 1973. They quickly found that Europe was different, the complication being the customs formalities required at the international borders. After three years and huge losses, TNT decided that they should concentrate on services within the UK, so a Lancashire based company with 500 employees was purchased.

The fast growth and the different overseas conditions were a financial challenge and in 1977/78 profits fell for the first time since its public incorpora-
tion in 1961. In 1980 the services in the UK were profitable and expanding
and TNT was listed on the London stock exchange. The UK and Europe was
to be the centre of TNT's expansion.

In 1979, the Ansett battle was on again. Sir Henry Bolte was no longer Premier
of Victoria, and there was a more liberalized corporate climate, so others were
buying Ansett shares. TNT decided to add to their existing shareholding and
bought more shares. When they found that News Corporation Ltd also had a
substantial holding, TNT and News agreed that they become the joint owners
of Ansett, each with 50% of the shares. Peter Abeles and Rupert Murdoch
became joint managing directors.

During the 1980s the UK operations grew quite quickly. TNT had their own
aircraft, several BAE QT146, and they enabled a guaranteed overnight service
to Scotland, Ireland and the offshore islands. The UK Post Office was told in
1982 that the TNT private parcel service would become a serious threat to the
Post Office parcels service.

In 1985, the company changed its name from Thomas Nationwide Transport
Ltd, to TNT Ltd.

There was a big boost to the UK operations in 1986. News Corporation owned
a number of newspapers printed in London and Rupert Murdoch wanted to
modernise their production. News Ltd built a new printing plant at Wapping,
a London suburb. The printing unions opposed this and Murdoch realised
that the rail unions would try to block the distribution of newspapers, a
job traditionally done by rail. Rupert Murdoch secretly gave his friend, and
Ansett colleague, Peter Abeles the distribution job. Trucks were prepared,

and 550 drivers recruited in one weekend; the unions were outsmarted and TNT had a major boost to their business.

By 1987 TNT had a firm hold in the United Kingdom, with 2200 trucks on the road. The European Union was coming; that meant more trade, more transport need, and more services were offered. TNT was operating in Eastern Europe, with air freight ventures with the Russian airline Aeroflot and Yugoslavia's JAT.

In September 1987, TNT was one of Australia's top 20 companies. The share price was very close to $6. Sir Peter Abeles rewarded himself with a salary that year of $5.35 million. On that share price the company was worth about $10 billion. Then came the stock market crash of October 1987. Unlike many of its peers, TNT failed to rebound after the crash.

In 1989, TNT encountered a major problem. In Australia there was an airline pilots' mass resignation after a salary dispute. Ansett, Australian Airlines (formally TAA), East West Airlines and IPEC, all had to rebuild their pilot force with new contracts, and that took months. Ansett was estimated to be losing $10 million each week. TNT's profits for the September quarter were down 70% on the previous year.

This coincided with financial problems in other countries too, and there was doubt about TNT's ability to survive in tough times. Their share price on the Australian stock exchange dropped to a record low in January 1991 of 75 cents. The company lost $90 million in the nine months to March 1991.

In July 1991 TNT announced a 50/50 joint venture with GD Net BV. This was a company owned by the post offices of five countries: Germany, France, The Netherlands, Sweden and Canada. The new arrangement was effective from October 1991. It was to be known as GD Express World Wide.

In 1992 things got worse. There were massive losses in Europe, and TNT shares fell to 55 cents. There was a boardroom coup, and Sir Peter was asked to resign as managing director. David Mortimer, the finance director was elevated to the managing director's office. Sir Peter would not let go, and developed a plan to unhook the European operations to eliminate the company's debt, which was rejected by the board in a long and bitter meeting in August 1993. Peter was asked to resign from the board.

David Mortimer had the job of cleaning up the problems. The Ansett shares were sold, and other non-core assets were on sale. The GD Express operation was starting to be profitable and was seen to be a good decision.

In October 1996, a takeover offer was made to TNT by a Dutch company KPN. The offer was $2.45 a share, a total price of $2 billion. The offer was 80 cents a share more than the last trading price.

KPN was a telecommunications and postal group; the TNT board unanimously agreed it was an attractive offer, and they would support the sale. There were then 8000 Australian employees, and KPN had indicated it wanted to integrate the TNT operations with their fast freight and parcel delivery services in 47 countries. That left the general freight transport services of TNT out of the picture.

In October 1997, Toll Holdings Ltd, paid $145 million for the general transport companies from TNT. The businesses sold were Carpentaria Transport, TNT Seafast, Refrigerated Roadways, TNT Port Logistics, TNT Bulk, TNT Container Express, TNT Integrated Logistics, and TNT Energy Logistics. Those companies represented about a third of TNT's Australian assets.

TNT announced that they intended to concentrate on the time sensitive domestic and international distribution operations, international mail and value added logistics. The companies to be developed under TNT's new strategy were, TNT Express Couriers, Comet, Kwikasair, McPhee Transport, Riteway Transport, TNT Express Worldwide, Mail Fast, TNT Automotive Logistics, and TNT Pallecons.

The Managing Director of Toll, Mr Paul Little, welcomed the chance to enhance Toll's logistics capabilities, and to keep the ownership of these companies in Australian hands.

The majority of TNT's Australian employees found themselves working for the Toll group.

Sir Peter Abeles died on 25th June 1999, aged 75.

In 2012, the directors of TNT received an offer to sell to the world wide UPS group. The offer was accepted, but was subject to various approvals. UPS was not strong in Australia, and the TNT profitable business would fill that gap. The TNT name would be lost.

In January 2013, the European competition regulator ruled that such an arrangement was not acceptable and the whole plan was abandoned.

ROAD TRANSPORT HISTORICAL SOCIETY

Australians who have made a contribution to the Road Transport Industry are the focus of the Hall of Fame at Alice Springs. This is the museum of the Road Transport Historical Society.

Why Alice Springs? The unusual location is the secret of both its existence and its success.

The Northern Territory presented some huge challenges to the need for transport. The early needs were met by camel trains, and when motor vehicles appeared in the early 20th century years, they gradually took over from the camels. The long distances, lack of roads, hot dry conditions, or wet season floods were all daily challenges for the battling pioneer road operators.

Those conditions meant the trucks were not normal. They were quickly rebuilt, added to and modified to do the job. There were some imports of special vehicles, and the powerful trucks became the motive for road trains, a world-wide first.

These pioneers, mostly men but a few women, and their unique vehicles were wearing out in the 1970s and 1980s, and the farsighted of them realised the history needed to be recorded while there was still time. So they decided to act.

This is where Territorians are different. In other places there would be a request for the government to do something, and then years of battling with politicians, public servants and advisors and little progress. In the territory they just pick up their tools and do it themselves.

One of the visionaries was Kurt Johannsen, owner of two iconic trucks: 'Bertha' and 'The Wog' both a Diamond T-180. Kurt made the first donation, and he cajoled a few truckie friends to get going.

Initially it was to be a Northern Territory Museum, but when people from Australia-wide took an interest and wanted to donate old vehicles, it became an Australian Road Transport Historical Institution. Its location in the centre of the continent is very appropriate.

Support has come from many people, companies and the transport industry, and the Alice Springs location is an important part of the appeal. Every year hundreds of nomadic grey hairs park their caravans behind the museum and work hard doing all sorts of tasks as volunteers. Many of them have little prior experience of the transport industry.

The road transport section includes hundreds of vehicles, from brand new Kenworths to older worn out vehicles, some restored and all historic in their own way. There are display halls with photos, and all sorts of memorabilia. A new library and resource centre has been built recently. Those who have been accepted into the hall of fame are remembered with a display panel. Right next door is the rail section, a museum of the Ghan train and the old line from the south.

To have grown so fast from a dream 20 years ago to its current status is thanks to many people, but the CEO, Liz Martin has been involved from the start, and has led the way. Liz has had a lifetime of living in the Northern Territory and being involved with transport.

ABOUT THE AUTHOR

David Wilcox has had an interest in transport since boyhood. The first 15 years of his business career were in the transport industry. Initially this was in the overseas passenger services of P&O, and their Australian agents, Macdonald Hamilton and Co.

In the mid 1950s David saw the coming decline in the passenger liner service as airlines developed, so considered his career options. The Hughes and Vale decision prompted a move to road transport, and a trainee position at Mayne Nickless. At age 21 he was their first general freight salesman in Sydney. From there he went to F.H.Stephens, and in due course was their NSW sales manager.

David was in the initial class of the Transport Administration Course offered by the Sydney Technical College. He graduated and became a member of the Institute Of Transport in 1958.

For family reasons he left the industry and spent 36 years, mainly in self-employment, at Crescent Head.

Now retired, he has had the time to indulge in his passion with transport to do the research and to write this, his first book.

David lives at Blackalls Park, Lake Macquarie, NSW.

www.ingramcontent.com/pod-product-compliance
Lightning Source LLC
Chambersburg PA
CBHW060002100426
42740CB00010B/1369